WITHDRAWN

SET YOURSELF UP
TO SELF-PUBLISH

D0879418

Other books by the author:

Publish Your Genealogy: A Step-by-Step Guide for Preserving Your Research for the Next Generation

Publish Your Family History: A Step-by-Step Guide to Writing the Stories of Your Ancestors

Publish a Local History: A Step-by-Step Guide from Finding the Right Project to Finished Book

Publish a Memoir: A Step-by-Step Guide to Saving Your Memories for Future Generations

Publish a Biography: A Step-by-Step Guide to Capturing the Life and Times of an Ancestor or a Generation

Publish a Photo Book: A Step-by-Step Guide for Transforming Your Genealogical Research into a Stunning Family Heirloom

Publish a Source Index: A Step-by-Step Guide to Creating a Genealogically-Useful Index, Abstract or Transcription

Publish Your Specialty: A Step-by-Step Guide for Imparting Your Research Expertise to Others

Set Yourself Up to Self-Publish

A Genealogist's Guide

by Dina C. Carson

Iron Gate Publishing
Niwot, CO

Set Yourself Up to Self-Publish:

A Genealogist's Guide

by Dina C. Carson

Published by:

Iron Gate Publishing
P.O. Box 999
Niwot, CO 80544

All rights reserved. No part of this book may be reproduced or transmitted in any form or by any means, electronic or mechanical, including photocopying, recording or any information storage and retrieval system without written permission from the author, except for the inclusion of brief quotations in a review.

Iron Gate Publishing has used its best efforts in collecting and preparing material for inclusion in *Set Yourself Up to Self-Publish: A Genealogist's Guide*, but does not warrant that the information herein is complete or accurate, and does not assume, and hereby disclaims, any liability to any person for any loss or damage caused by errors or omissions in *Set Yourself Up to Self-Publish: A Genealogist's Guide*, whether such errors or omissions result from negligence, accident or any other cause.

Copyright © 2014 by Dina C. Carson, Iron Gate Publishing
Printed in the United States of America
     ISBN   1-879579-99-5   ISBN 13 978-1-879579-99-6
     LCCN   2014914860

Publisher's Cataloging-in-Publication Data

Carson, Dina C, 1961 -

    Set Yourself Up to Self-Publish: A Genealogist's Guide
by Dina C Carson.

             p.   cm.
    Includes index.
    ISBN 978-1-879579-99-6 (softbound) $24.95

      1. Self-Publishing—United States
2. Language Arts & Disciplines—Publishing.
3. Reference—Writing.   I. Title.

CT5. C239 2014   [Z285.5 G46 C37 2014 -- Self-Publishing]
070.593

Dedicated to my family,
without whose love and guidance,
I may have become a politician.

Acknowledgments

My kindest, most deeply held thanks to:

Dad—who supported my every effort in genealogy and loved hearing about every find I ever made.

Mom—who had enough patience to read every word in this series of books and made each book better.

Charly Miller—whose Harry Potter Places travel guides have charmed me through and through, and who has supported every last thing I have done to make these books possible.

Buzzy Jackson—who wrote the stories of her ancestors in an enviable way, and was kind enough to lend her expertise to launch this project.

Silvia Pettem—whose remarkable local histories encourage me and so many others to poke about Boulder and write about our discoveries.

Dr. Thomas W. Jones—whose kind words and brilliant edits inspired me to share what I know about publishing.

Pat Roberts and Mona Lambrecht—who inspired an entire workshop on writing, research and publishing that lead directly to this series of books.

Sandi Pearce—my grammar goddess, who keeps me from tumbling headlong over my own words.

Gena Philibert-Ortega—for the most amazing week of social history studies. I have never had so much fun in a class.

Dr. John Philip Colletta—for providing the inspiration to take the next step and finish these books.

My friends at the Boulder Genealogical Society, the JGSCO, the Boulder Heritage Roundtable, and the Colorado Council of Genealogical Societies—who have encouraged me to write, to lecture, and through steadfast community spirit have kept me going.

Because ...

*" ... we may find ourselves bedeviled by a weak link
in a future generation willing to throw things out
without checking what it is first."*

—Carl Boyer

How to Publish and Market Your Family History

Updates

Websites come and go or change how they are structured. If you find a broken link or a website that has moved or changed its name, please help me update the book for the next generation of readers. Send an email to: alert@irongate.com.

Contents

SECTION 5: PROFESSIONAL ASSISTANCE

Preface

I started publishing in 1989 before self-publishing became popular or quite so easy. The reason I did so was because a friend and I were working on a series of books about planning reunions, and we wanted to know what our options were to publish the books. Back then, we found plenty of options, but few good options.

Non-fiction books enjoy the advantage of having an an easily identifiable audience, but are disadvantaged due to lack of interest by publishers or bookstores for selling a few books here and there, even if an audience is clamoring for the information contained in the book. It turns out that you are better off publishing some non-fiction books yourself.

Enter Dan Poynter and his *Self-Publishing Manual: How to Write, Print and Sell Your Own Book*. Tom and Marilyn Ross were not far behind with *The Complete Guide to Self-Publishing*. I learned from their books, I attended publishing conferences and joined publishers groups. I endured the pain of writing an enormous check to the printer for which I received eight pallets of books stacked four feet high, numbering more than 10,000 books. It is harder than you think to sell 10,000 books, but it can be done. Thankfully, these days, there is almost never a need for 10,000 books in one delivery unless you have a blockbuster on your hands. A blockbuster is a good problem to have.

The best news for genealogists and family historians is the ease with which self-publishing takes place today. You will notice that I did not say that the research or writing was easy, or that laying out and typesetting a manuscript was easy. Once you have a manuscript ready for print, however, the actual process of choosing a printer, uploading the files, and having a single book delivered to your doorstep at a reasonable cost, is E A S Y.

Throughout this book, I will remind you that if you can do the research, you *can* publish. If you can crawl through the depths of Aunt Mabel's basement in a quest for the family bible, if you can schlep your toddler to the Family History Library in Salt Lake, if you can endure a sweltering Missouri courthouse attic in August, you can self-publish.

I have written this book in a conversational style—just us having a conversation, sharing what I know. My primary aim is to take the fear out of the process—to put your mind at ease—by helping you recognize that after researching and writing a fantastic family history, there is no reason for you to stumble over the last step, publishing the book.

Set Yourself Up to Self-Publish: A Genealogist's Guide is the first in a series of nine books that describes the process of publishing. The other books tackle the particulars of planning, research, writing and marketing the following:

- A genealogy—your research, published in order to pass it along to the next generation of researchers.
- A family history—your family stories, based upon the research, written so that your non-genealogical relatives will enjoy reading it.
- A local history—everything from the history of a region to the stories of a single farm or business.
- A memoir—the story of you, told for a future generation.
- A biography—focusing less on an entire family and more on an individual or couple.
- A photo book—fewer stories, fantastic images.
- A source index—indexing record sets, the bedrock on which genealogical research stands.
- A how-to—imparting your research expertise to help others.

For now, allow me to explain your options for publishing in print, electronically, and online.

Introduction

Throughout this book, you will read the words, "If you can do the research, you can publish it." Why? Because I truly believe it.

Before we move to the nuts and bolts of page layout and typesetting, I want to explain to you what your options are for publishing.

You can publish in print, and there are plenty of publishing companies out there to do that for you, if you choose. I believe, however, that there are many advantages to self-publishing. So many, in fact, that most family historians choose the self-publishing route.

You can publish electronically. There is something appealing about being able to send your cousins a copy of the book without incurring any expenses to print and ship. About one quarter of adult readers have switched to electronic devices (eReaders or tablets) on which to read books. Many of these people do not buy books in print any longer. Fortunately, the process of converting a book you have laid out for print is fairly simple. Once you have the print manuscript ready, why not take a few extra steps and publish an eBook version as well?

You can publish online. Publishing online is an organizational challenge, but has the benefit of making your book available across the globe to anyone who wants to read it.

Section One describes the stages of a publishing project, how to pick a project that is doable, how traditional and self-publishing works, and the tools that facilitate the job of typesetting and layout.

Section Two describes the ins and outs of print publishing. The books that look the best also are the easiest on the eyes to read. Reading comprehension decreases dramatically when books are not typeset well. Books that are not typeset well also look amateurish. This section will give you all of the instructions you need to make your book look its best.

Section Three describes the steps necessary to turn your print manuscript into an electronic book and to add some interactivity, if you wish.

Section Four describes how to overcome the organizational challenges that accompany online publishing using a website, a blog or social media.

Section Five is useful if you do not want to tackle the entire publishing project yourself and require professional assistance to:

- Scan your images and prepare them for use in your book
- Photograph objects, people or places
- Hire an illustrator for one-of-a-kind artwork
- Work with a cover designer, book packager or indexer

My original contention bears repeating. If you can research, you *can* publish.

SECTION 1

The goal in this section is to give you enough of an understanding about how publishing works to make you comfortable with the decision to self-publish.

First, we will take a look at the stages of all publishing projects—planning, writing, production and marketing.

Then, you will see how traditional book publishing works, and how everything a traditional publisher could do for you, you can do quite easily for yourself.

Finally, we will examine the tools you will need to make your way from bright idea to a book in your hands.

Keep reading. If you have ancestors who are interesting enough to research, they have stories interesting enough to tell.

Chapter 1

Why Self-Publish?

With a little bit of knowledge, you can take your research and make it available to family, friends or other researchers in print, as an electronic book, or online. If you can do the research, you can also do the publishing. Modern publishing technology makes it possible for anyone to create a quality, published family history.

Not only will family members appreciate knowing more about their heritage, the hours you spent researching deserves to become an everlasting record of your family's history. Self-publishing is one way to assure the legacy of your research.

Who Needs This Book?

You need this book if you:
- are still gathering research, but want to know what your publishing options are.
- do not want to pay for and store a garage full of books produced the old-fashioned way in print runs of hundreds.
- are already planning a publishing project and need to know what the next step is.
- want to issue a private publication available only to you or your immediate family members, so you can write about living people without worrying about privacy issues.
- want to share what only *you* have access to, such as one-of-a-kind photographs, letters, the family bible or heirlooms.
- are ready to gather photographs, but need some basic instruction about creating digital images.
- are scratching your head about ISBNs.

- have no idea what it takes to create an eBook, or how to deliver an electronic book to interested readers.
- have not considered publishing online because you did not know that was possible.

Where Do You Start?

Have you ever said to yourself, "I'll write a book when the research is done?"

Many of us—yes, myself included—could pitch a tent at the National Archives and still not gather every source we desire. There is *always* another graveyard to find or courthouse to search. At some point, we need to put aside the quest for *every* ancestor, and focus on a few—just long enough to write their stories down so the reason we did the research in the first place is not lost.

Kirk Polking, in his book *Writing Family Histories and Memoirs,* describes a woman who entered a "Why am I a Writer?" contest. Her answer to that question was that she read about a man who had always wanted to be an artist. After he died, his house was filled with pots of paint and empty canvases. On the day she read that story, she put pen to paper with all of the thoughts she had been saving up for that *someday* when she would be a writer.

That day has come.

Where do *you* start? You start by learning about the publishing process.

Chapter 2

Publishing Projects—
The Four Stages

Every publishing project, whether it is a family history or the next blockbuster novel, goes through four stages—planning, writing, production and marketing.

Planning

The first step in any publishing project is the planning stage, where you decide what type of book to write—how much to include or how little. If you think you must include every family you have researched in a single volume, you do not.

In fact, I want discourage the data dump—purging your family history software of every available name and source you have into one enormous manuscript. It may feel good to see how much research you have already done. But once you start adding the images and the historical or social context to numerous family lines, the project may become overwhelming.

Choose a single ancestor or a single generation to write about, more like a biography; or limit the book to two generations plus the collateral lines. Maybe you have three generations who stayed in one place whose collective history is interesting. Perhaps a hybrid family and local history is more to your liking.

In Chapter 3: Pick a Project to Publish, we will explore many different ways you can publish the research you already have. The possibilities are endless.

Writing

The writing stage is perhaps the most feared part of the publishing process. All writers face that first blank page. All writers have doubts. "What if I can't think of anything to say? What if I don't like what I've written? What if no one else likes what I've written?"

Anxiety about writing is completely normal. Thankfully, the writing stage is not all writing. For most family historians, it is a writing and research stage. Research, for many of us, is a much more comfortable, more familiar place. Feel free to retreat into the comfort zone every now and again to gather material to strengthen your stories. Be wary of letting a small detour back into the research become an excuse to avoid writing. Eventually, you will want to finish the book.

Once the manuscript is complete, you must edit. Not even the most accomplished writer can produce a perfect manuscript in the first draft. Editing always means fixing typos and catching errors. Editing often means rewriting. Editing will make your manuscript better, more enjoyable for the reader.

Production

During the production stage, you will design the look and style of the book, *and* follow a set of rules to make the book easy to read.

Production decisions include page layout, image placement, typesetting, cover design and final files. Fear not. There are ample software tools to help you lay out the pages and make the images look their best.

During the production phase, you will decide whether to produce the book solely in print, whether an electronic or an online format may be better, or perhaps some combination of all three.

Once you have a book in hand, your work is not quite done. The final stage of any publishing project is marketing.

Marketing

Marketing is not necessarily about generating sales. It is a means of letting people who have an interest in your ancestors know that the book is available. You may choose to give the book away to siblings and cousins as gifts. You may want to conduct a private sale, so only close family members can obtain a copy. You may want to sell the book to avoid financing the entire production yourself. Or, you may have a book with broader appeal that would warrant a sales campaign.

Marketing a family history is a long-term process because family histories do not go out of style and should not go out of print. The most important part of marketing is letting family members and other researchers know that your book is available.

None of these stages has nice, neat beginnings and endings. Occasionally, you may need to return to the planning to gather more information to make the writing easier. You may discover errors or missing elements while you are typesetting that initiate a re-write. Even with a finished book, during the marketing stage you may discover some piece of blockbuster information that demands a second edition or a new book.

No family history will roll off the press complete or perfect. Time ticks on. Families change. New information comes to light. Expect it and publish anyway.

Chapter 3

Pick a Project to Publish

The most important consideration for your publishing project is that you are able to complete it. Part of the fun of family history is that it is never done. There will always be a new discovery or another baby born. The challenge for you, right now, is to pick a part of your research that you are willing to focus on to the exclusion of other interesting finds, and narrow the scope enough that the project does not become overwhelming.

In the meantime, let us explore a few ideas in more detail.

A Family History

What is the difference between a genealogy and a family history?

In technical terms, a *genealogy* begins with an ancestor and moves forward in time through his or her descendants. A *pedigree*, on the other hand, starts with a descendant and moves backward through the ancestors.

For our purposes, consider a **genealogy** a way to pass on your well-documented *research* (with or without a lot of narrative). A **family history**, on the other hand, is less a numbered lineage but rather the *stories* of your ancestors.

The challenge with any family history project is limiting the scope enough that you can tell the stories well. One consideration is the time period in which the chosen family lived. For your own generation, you have personal knowledge of the people and can tell their stories from your experience. And, most probably, there are hundreds if not thousands of photographs for you to choose from to help you remember events in order to write about them and help illustrate the stories once they are written.

To write about the generation before you, you may know each family member, or you may need to consult other family members for their stories. For your grandparents' generation (and further back), you may not have as many people to consult or as many photographs to look at. Once you get back beyond the Civil War era, you may not have any photographs at all. At some point in the past, you will be relying entirely upon research.

The following are ideas for planning a family history:

Start to Finish. Pick the ancestor you wish to use as the first generation. Describe the circumstances of that ancestor's entry into the family—not necessarily his or her birth, rather setting the scene for his or her early years. Follow the family through the number of generations you have chosen to include describing the events that affect most families—the births, schooling, marriages, professions and deaths. Add the migrations, moves or turns of events that happened to your family. Enrich the stories with enough social history so that the reader understands what it was like to live in the time and place your ancestors lived.

Photographs or Memorabilia. If you have inherited a box of photographs or memorabilia, plan your project around the people, places and events you find in that collection.

Letters or a Diary. Write about the people or person who wrote the letters or diary, weaving the actual text into the stories, or using the events described as the time line for the book.

A Tragedy. Write about a defining event that affected the family, such as a natural disaster, the death of a child, becoming a prisoner of war, losing a fortune, or surviving the Great Depression or the Holocaust.

A Triumph. Triumphs are also defining events, such as suddenly becoming very wealthy, becoming famous, being elected to an important office, and so on.

An Ancestor and the People Known to Him or Her. A book of this type could include parents, siblings, grandparents, children and grandchildren, cousins, aunts and uncles—essentially five generations—the two before and the two following your main character.

A Single Generation. If you are going to focus on an individual or a couple (e.g. your parents or grandparents), consult, *Publish a Biography: A Step-by-Step Guide to Capturing the Life and Times of an Ancestor or a Generation*. The difference is mostly in the level of detail required.

If you have done the research and are ready to write the stories, consult, *Publish Your Family History: A Step-by-Step Guide to Writing the Stories of Your Ancestors.*

A Genealogy

By my definition, a genealogy is a little less about writing and a little more about passing along your research to other researchers. For those of you have plenty of research to choose from, but are not quite ready to write the stories, publishing a genealogy will give you experience with the publishing process. Publishing your research is a valuable effort, in an of itself.

The following are ideas for planning a genealogy:

Every Descendant of a Single Ancestor. That may be your grandparents, or the first immigrant. The more generations you go back, the more challenging it will be to ensure that the lines are complete.

Direct Descendants of a Single Ancestor. Include the siblings in each generation, but the detailed information only for your direct line.

Female Lines. Your mother, and her mother, and her mother, and so on, as far back as you have researched.

A Surname Line. Beginning with the first ancestor of a given surname (a female), following her surname (male) line backward. Another section of the book could include the wives of the male ancestors as collateral lines.

A Direct Line to a Specific Ancestor. Beginning with yourself, you could trace back across different surnames to a specific ancestor, such as an American President or a Salem witch. This is the kind of research commonly done to join a lineage society.

A Surname Study. Focus on a surname in a particular region (e.g. The Bakers of Campbell County, KY), or within a national database (e.g. Revolutionary War soldiers or patriots), or across a complete record set (e.g. federal census records).

If you have done the research, but are not quite ready to write the narrative, consult, *Publish Your Genealogy: A Step-by-Step Guide for Preserving Your Research for the Next Generation.*

A Local History

There are endless possibilities for writing local histories. All families have elements of local history in their stories. Right? They attended local schools, worked in local businesses, joined community organizations, participated in local government and some lived in neighborhoods.

The following are ideas for elements of local history to enhance your family history. Any of these ideas could become a local history unto itself:

Professions. Farming, mining, ranching, medicine, crafts, craftsmanship, banking, manufacturing, logging, science, technology, information, inventions, merchants, wholesalers, working conditions ...

Institutions. Schools, courts, military units, libraries, government agencies, fire departments, law and order ...

Associations. Sports teams, Masons, Odd Fellows, Boy Scouts, Girl Scouts, 4H, philanthropic, social, fraternal, activist ...

Religious Groups. Church, synagogues, mosques, religious movements ...

Transportation. Freighters, wagon roads, railroads, stage companies, stations or airports, river boats, barges, trails or roads, aerospace, aeronautics ...

People. Famous or notorious, leaders, office holders, women, children, what became of (e.g. a school class), the poor, ethnic groups, religious groups ...

Events. Natural disasters, on this day, during this year, anniversaries, economic depression, loss or gain of a major employer, politics ...

Architecture. Neighborhoods, downtown, building styles, building techniques, public buildings, historic homes ...

Transitions. Town into city, fort into town, farm into metropolis ...

Customs. Marriage, burial, holidays, celebrations, 4th of July, parades, rallies, expectations, manners, roles for men, women, and children, economic class ...

Entertainment. Music, art, dance, theater, movies, plays, books, leisure ...

If you are considering writing a local history, consult, *Publish a Local History: A Step-by-Step Guide from Finding the Right Project to Finished Book.*

A Photo Book

There are some family stories best told by focusing on the photographs or illustrations with snippets of text to accompany the images.

The following are ideas for family picture books or pictorial histories:

Heirloom Catalog. You may have family heirlooms that could be shared in pictures. This is one way to preserve the many historical items that belong to your family, even if they have been scattered across the globe, and showcase them in a book.

Holiday Traditions. Maybe you have Christmas cards or letters saved over the years that could accompany yearly pictures. Or, perhaps you have photos of other holidays your family regularly celebrates that would make a good transition-through-time journal.

School Pictures. Starting in the 1950s, most school children had individual photographs taken each year as well as a class picture. Here is one way to show what the family was doing every year across a decade or a generation.

Themes. Does your family have something in common? Eye or hair color? Freckles or jawline? Hobbies? Can you find a picture of different members of the family with their bikes, while skiing or fishing? Maybe you have a collection of wedding photographs across the generations.

Travel Diary. If you have made the trip of a lifetime, or a trip to research your family's origins, show your family what the old country looked like through your modern-day experiences and photographs.

Preservation. If you have a photo album or scrapbook made by one of your family members, preserve it by creating a more modern edition while adding stories gleaned from interviews or research.

Letters Home. Maybe you have letters from a soldier written to those at home during a war, or from a student who traveled abroad.

Talents. Was your grandmother a knitter or did she tat? Do you have examples of her work that would make a good pictorial history? Maybe your family's talent was acting or painting, scroll work or whittling, jewelry or quilting?

If you are considering a picture history consult, *Publish a Photo Book: A Step-by-Step Guide for Transforming Your Genealogical Research into a Stunning Family Heirloom*, for more details on image preparation in full color.

A Biography

A biography is different from a family history in that it focuses on an individual or a couple rather than trying to follow a family across generations. A biography requires a greater level of detail about people including where they lived, the era they lived in, what kind of schooling they had, associations they joined, and how they worked.

The following are ideas for family biographies:

Parent(s) or Grandparent(s). These are people you may have the most information about, persons you know or knew well. This book could be a tribute to a couple or an individual.

Famous Ancestor. Whether famous or *notorious*, did your ancestor participate in a well-known historical event? Was he or she a professional athlete, or famous entertainer? Did he or she establish a town, or start a business?

Interesting Profession. Maybe you had an ancestor who was a hatter, a furniture maker, or a smelter. Maybe your ancestor was an inventor who changed the lives of many people? Researching how an ancestor worked may be interesting to other people whose ancestors held similar jobs.

If you are interested in writing a biography, consult: *Publish a Biography: A Step-by-Step Guide to Capturing the Life and Times of an Ancestor or a Generation.*

A Memoir

While it may seem a strange exercise for family historians to do research on yourself or your generation, telling your story should not be. A generation from now, your children or grandchildren will be interested in how you lived.

The following are ideas for writing a memoir:

An Aspect of Your Life. Pick a part of your lifespan to write about—childhood, teenage years, college experiences, married life.

Professional Life. Perhaps it is your work life that you would most like to write about.

Military Life. Even if you did not choose the military as a profession, tell the stories of your experience in the service—during peacetime or at war.

Remembrances. If you have greeting cards or letters that help tell your story, consider weaving those into a memoir.

Journal or Diary. If you have kept a journal or diary, expand upon what you were thinking at the time you wrote the original entries.

Travel. If you have traveled extensively, create a lasting journal of the places you have gone, the experiences you had, the people you met along the way, and the things you saw.

If you are interested in writing a memoir, consult: *Publish a Memoir: A Step-by-Step Guide to Saving Your Memories for Future Generations.*

A How-To

If you have conducted extensive research in any one aspect of genealogy or local history, share your expertise with others. Everyone can benefit when we help each other avoid the pitfalls of conducting family history research.

The following are a ideas for how-to books:

Tips and Tricks. You could give snippets of advice for people who are new to an area of research.

Process. Describe how to do something from start to finish. Here is where your knowledge of an earlier time may help readers understand what their ancestors did and how they did it. How were houses constructed in the 17th Century? How did hunters keep enough food on the table at a western fort? How did Paul Revere make copper-bottomed pans?

Lessons Learned. Reveal the techniques that did not work in your research so others can avoid making the same mistakes.

Record Type. You may have experience in land records or military records, for example, and can help others use those records in their own research.

Research Facility. Perhaps you have shortcuts to share about making the best use of your time at a major repository, or perhaps shine a light on a repository that few researchers know about.

Recording or Preserving Records. Do you have photography tips for taking the best travel or cemetery pictures to use in a family history book, or advice for best practices to preserve the family bible?

Location. You may have conducted extensive research in a particular location and could create a guide to what is available there.

If you are interested in writing a how-to book, consult: *Publish Your Specialty: A Step-by-Step Guide for Imparting Your Research Expertise to Others.*

A Source Index

Recently, I heard a speaker state that only two percent of all the material that could be digitized has been digitized, which makes me think that good records extractions will be necessary for a long time to come. If nothing else, creating an index that makes a record set easier to use is a valuable gift to other genealogists.

There is no limit to the places where records are kept: government (e.g. schools, agencies, cities, counties, etc.); company (e.g. mortuary, ditch companies, banks, merchants, etc.); associations (e.g. religious groups, Masons, Odd

Fellows, service clubs, philanthropic clubs, community groups, sports teams, etc.); publications (e.g. journals, newspapers, etc.), transportation (e.g. trains, freighters, ships, planes, etc.), cemeteries (e.g. headstone transcriptions, lot purchasers, burial certificates, etc.) ... to name a few.

The following are ideas for records extractions:

An Index. If you are in the records anyway, you may as well do a thorough job and collect every name, every subject and every location. In addition to record sets, many 19th Century local histories could use an index.

An Annotated Index. If you want to take an index one step further, you could add useful information such as the role each individual played within the records (e.g. juror, judge or witness) and the date each event occurred.

An Abstract. Without going as far as a full transcription, you could abstract the basic points of court cases, probate files, or meeting minutes.

A Transcription. While our first duty is to do no harm to the archive that holds the records, you can write a transcription in a way that still encourages readers to visit the archive to obtain copies of the original records, so that the collection does not become less valuable as a result of your transcription.

An Annotated Transcription. You may be familiar enough with the records, or the people whose names appear in the records, that you could add information to make the transcription more valuable to the reader.

Preservation Plus Extraction. Some records are so fragile that they are difficult to use without damaging them. In this case, photograph the records so they can be shown in the book in their original form along with an index, an abstraction, or a complete transcription.

A Comprehensive Index. Consider indexing each source within a single collection (e.g. California gold rush participants in the Bancroft Collection), or across many collections to create a comprehensive index (e.g. Boulder Pioneers in the Colorado State Archives).

If you are interested in publishing a source index, consult: *Publish a Source Index: A Step-by-Step Guide to Creating a Genealogically-Useful Index, Abstract or Transcription.*

Hybrid Projects

You may have a project in mind that does not fit neatly into any one category. Your book does not have to. Be creative with some hybrid ideas.

The following are a few of the many possibilities for a hybrid family history:

Biography/Cookbook. While you write a biography, include a few recipes or family traditions sprinkled through the text.

Cookbook/Biography. Organize this one as a cookbook, but include some biographical information about the people who contributed the recipes, or how the recipes were used in family traditions.

Biography/Professional Manual. You may have enough information about an ancestor's work to compile a professional guide or work process history along with biographical information.

Photographic Time Line. Show how each family member fits into the photographic tree, or how they fit into the time line of history.

Memoir/History. Use recollections from a memoir, letters or a diary, alongside the real-world history taking place.

Travel Guide/Family History. Let your family members follow your footsteps as you traveled to the homeland, along with information about the people who lived in the places you describe. You could also include travel guide information to help the reader make the trip, too.

Perpetual Calendar. Include birth and death dates, anniversaries, graduations, immigration, military service, travel—anything that puts living relatives or ancestors on the calendar.

On This Day. Place historical events from your family history research or a local history into a day-by-day collection.

Genealogical Gifts

While books are the most appreciated gifts according to reunion-goers, there are many other ways to give away your genealogical research as gifts.

The following are a few of the many possibilities for genealogical gifts:

Charts. There is software available to help you create phenomenal family tree charts—fan charts, half-circles, full circles, or bow-tie charts. You can add photographs or background images, and information in great detail.

Scrapbooks. There are books, clubs and stores devoted to creating amazing scrapbooks. If you can picture it as a pedigree, you can scrapbook it in a way that shows family relationships.

Photographs on Products. You can put a photograph on nearly anything—cakes, wall hangings, button covers, place mats, cups, mugs, t-shirts, ornaments, wooden blocks, tote bags, candles, puzzles, window clings, calendars, key chains, coasters, journals, aprons, magnets, buttons, flip flops, or golf balls.

Cookbooks. There are companies that specialize in producing cookbooks since so many groups use them as fundraisers. Use your next holiday or reunion to gather up the family's favorite recipes.

Card Decks. There are companies that specialize in playing card decks that you can create using photographs of your family. Sports cards are another idea along the same line.

Quilts. Quilting was one way to re-use scrap material and create a warm blanket before there was central heating. Quilting patterns can reveal something about your ancestors' ethnic heritage or the area where they lived. Other textiles such as tartans have similar meanings to family groups.

Replica Items. You may find a replica item of something your ancestors owned or could have owned that may be a meaningful gift. Look in historical museum catalogs for these items.

Slide Show. There is software to help you gather photographs and add captions for a slide show that you can distribute or place online for your family to see.

Now that you have a great many ideas for turning your genealogical research into a book, let us look at how publishing works to determine the easiest way for you to finish your book and make it available to interested family members.

Chapter 4

How Publishing Works

Publishing has two essential parts—production and distribution. Before you determine whether to publish your book in print, electronically, or online, think about how your audience will want to read the book, and how you are going to deliver it to them.

It is hard to go wrong choosing print. The upside is that nearly everyone is able to read a printed book. The downside is that printed books must be produced and distributed (shipped) which cost money. Thankfully, print-on-demand technology has made it possible to print and ship books one at a time. Gone are the days when you had to order hundreds of books to keep the cost of each book down.

Publishing in an electronic format is tempting because there is almost no cost of production or distribution. Books can be sent to the reader electronically. The downside to electronic formats is that not everyone wants to read a book on a computer screen, dedicated eReader or tablet.

Publishing online is also tempting because most people have access to the Internet. Anyone with a web browser can read the book. The downside is that Internet companies come and go, so if your book is sitting on the server of a company that folds, the book disappears with it.

What is the best option for your book? You do not have to make a decision about this just yet. You may choose to publish in more than one format. Later in the book, I will give you work flow tips to make formatting for more than one publishing option easy.

Before we move on to production, let us look at publishing options in more detail.

Print Publishing

Before print-on-demand made publishing easy for anyone, there were four ways to publish a book in print. There still are. You could write a query letter to interest a traditional publishing company, pay a vanity publisher, hire a book packager, or self-publish. Before you decide to self-publish, here are the more traditional routes to book publishing and how they work.

Traditional Book Publishers

There are more than a few types of traditional publishers. There are the big publishers, such as Random House. Random House is one of the remaining Big Five, and companies such as this one are looking for the next blockbuster. They are not likely to be interested in a family history. There are also smaller publishers, mostly niche publishers, such as Arcadia Publishing that specializes in local history books.

In order to get the attention of one of the big publishers, you may need a literary agent to make the pitch to the company for you. Writing a good query letter introducing yourself and your book may work with a smaller publisher. Most family histories, unless they include someone famous or have a more general interest theme, will not interest a traditional publisher enough to offer you a contract.

Still, if you have a great family story to tell and can interest a publishing company, they will buy the rights to publish a version of your work (e.g. print, electronic, audio, foreign language, or all rights) in exchange for a royalty—a percentage of the sales price. Most publishing contracts are based upon the sales price rather than the retail price because so many books are sold at a steep discount to bookstores or book clubs.

When the book sells, the publisher is paid and they will handle any returns. You will be paid approximately ninety (90) days after the publisher, to allow time for returns.

A well-known author can expect a royalty of about fifteen percent, a lesser known author about ten percent, and an unknown family historian something less than ten percent. For most authors, a small percentage of the sales price (your royalty) means you have to sell a great number of books to make any money. For most family histories, this is not likely.

A traditional publisher will have total control over the physical production, distribution and sales. The publisher will choose the cover design. Oftentimes they will choose the title. Most importantly, they will control the content through the editing process. As the author, you will start the process, but once the contract is signed, the publisher is in control.

If your book needs revisions or corrections, that will only take place after the initial print run is sold. For many books, the first print run never sells out.

(One advantage to self-publishing using a print-on-demand printer is that you can make revisions at any time.)

A traditional publisher will decide how long the book will stay in print, and how long marketing will continue. For many books, once the sales slow, the marketing ends. (If you self-publish, the book will stay in print as long as you want it to.)

Vanity Publishers

You could enlist a vanity publisher to "publish" your book and "market" it to potential readers. Please do not. In reality, these companies are offering to take as much of your money as you are willing to give them, and do nothing for you that you could not do cheaper. It is best to avoid these companies all together. That goes for some author services companies, as well.

Book Packagers

Book packagers offer the different parts of the publishing process as services a-la-carte. If you do not want to handle the book cover design, for example, you could hire one of these companies to do so for you. You sign a contract for a specific service at a specific price. Book packagers can be helpful if you do not want to learn everything there is to know about book production but still want a professional looking book.

Author Services

Author services companies offer many of the same services that book packagers do, as well as editing and marketing. Some of the biggest print-on-demand printers also offer author services. CreateSpace (www.createspace.com) and its author services company BookSurge (www.booksurge.com), Lulu (www.lulu.com), and Blurb (www.blurb.com), offer packages of author services, such as copy editing, eBook conversion, layout, and cover design.

Most of the time, you will be able to do for yourself most of what they are offering to do for a fee. A better solution may be to find a local person, a book packager, who can design a cover or who can typeset the book for you at a fee you can negotiate, rather than having to accept a package price for more services than you want or need.

Caution: Author Solutions (www.authorsolutions.com) the author services provider of Penguin Random House (via its imprints AuthorHouse, Trafford, Booktango, WordClay, FuseFrame, PitchFest, Author Learning Center, Author Hive, Xlibris, Palibro, Inkubook, Patrtridge and iUniverse) had a federal class-action lawsuit filed against them in 2013 alleging that they have been cheating writers out of their royalties and charging outrageous prices for services—for years. What follows are the names of companies that have aligned themselves with Author Solutions. Please avoid these vanity presses: Archway (Simon & Schuster),

Partridge (Penguin), Westbow (Thomas Nelson/Harper Collins), Balboa Press (Hay House), Abbott Press (Writers' Digest), Dellarte Press (Harlequin). Many thanks to David Gaughran, author of *Let's Get Visible: How to Get Visible and Sell More Books* for helping fellow writers avoid trouble.

Self-Publishing

The best option for most family historians is self-publishing. You are your own publisher. You are in control of the whole process. You decide what goes into the book and how it looks. You control who can buy the book if there is information about living people you do not want out to the general public. You control the contents and the process. You also do most of the work. Fortunately, printing technology and software to create book layouts and electronic files has made self-publishing not only possible, but relatively easy.

Now that you have a better understanding of the role of the publisher, let us take a look at some of the nuts and bolts decisions about print production.

Book Printers

Please use a book printer, not the local copy shop. Producing books one at a time at the local copy shop will not only be expensive, but most copy shops do not have the kind of equipment to create books with permanent covers—either softbound (perfect bound) or hard-bound. The local copy shop may be good if your manuscript will only fill a booklet (under 48 pages) rather than a book, and if you only plan to print a limited number.

To create quality softbound or hard bound books, there are two options—print-on-demand or offset presses.

Offset Book Printers

Using an offset book printer has its advantages, especially if you can sell or give away a large print run. Ordering books in quantity will keep the price per book down. The downside is that you have to print and pay for a minimum number of books up front—often 250 or more.

Offset printing is best for books with custom sizes or books that require high-quality reproduction such as photography or coffee table books. High-quality, full-color books are often printed in Asia because the cost is lower, even with international shipping.

Print-on-Demand Book Printers

Print-on-demand (POD) book printers are exactly as their name suggests—you can print a single book when you need it. There is a wide variety of print-on-demand printers. The following is a representative example of what you will find.

Lulu

Lulu (www.lulu.com) is a POD book printer that also offers author and marketing services. Their business model assumes that you, the publisher, have no experience, so their website will guide you through the process step by step. Anyone can create a printed copy of a book through Lulu. The only downside is that there is no quality control during the process, and some (mostly people in the book industry) may assume that your book is amateurish if you publish through Lulu. If you are not worried about selling the book except to friends or family, then there is no need to worry about where you have your book printed. The ease of using Lulu's website is an attractive plus.

Lulu is one of the few POD book printers with privacy options. At Lulu, you can make the book available only to you or by private web link to only those people you allow to buy the book. This is an attractive option for proofing books and for keeping books out of the hands of the general public if they contain information about living people. There will undoubtedly be people in your family who will want complete information in your family history, but may be uncomfortable with making birth dates, for example, available to the public.

Lulu also has an online bookstore if you want to make your book available for sale. Lulu's catalog also appears in Amazon's catalog, although, both Lulu and Amazon will take a cut before you earn a royalty if you print your book through Lulu but sell it through Amazon.

At Lulu your wholesale prices may be higher than at other POD printers. If you are selling the book to make a little money, investigate other options.

CreateSpace

CreateSpace (www.createspace.com) is Amazon's POD printer. They expect you to know a little bit more about the process, so the website is not as easy to use as Lulu. CreateSpace will have a staff person review your book before approving it. Your book will not become available in the Amazon catalog without approval. This can be a hurdle if you have unusual page numbering or something that makes the staff unsure of the quality of the work.

The upside is that your book will be available at the largest online bookstore on the Internet and your wholesale prices will be lower at CreateSpace than they are at Lulu. Amazon's reach is enormous, meaning your book will be available literally around the world, if you print through CreateSpace.

Lightning Source

At the far end of the scale is Lightning Source (www.lightningsource.com). Lightning Source is an Ingram Company. Ingram is the largest book wholesaler in the United States, and selling through their catalog means access to 30,000 wholesalers, retailers and booksellers in more than one hundred countries around the world.

Lightning Source *only* works with publishers. They expect you have experience with the process.

At Lightning Source, you must have your own International Standard Book Numbers (ISBNs), unlike CreateSpace and Lulu—both offer free ISBNs. All books, including different versions of the same book (an eBook or a 2nd Edition must have an ISBN. ISBNs are like the Social Security number for a book. ISBNs distinguish one book from another, or a newer version from an older version. The benefit of a free ISBN is cost savings since a single ISBN costs $125.00. A package of 10 ISBNs costs $295.00; 100 ISBNs cost $575, and so on. The more you buy, the less they cost per ISBN. You can purchase ISBNs through the Bowker Company's Identifier Services (www.myidentifiers.com). Also, if you use a free ISBN from your printer, that company will become the publisher of record, not you.

Lightning Source charges fees to establish and maintain each book in their catalog. There are also fees for every update or revision. In other words, you need a next-to-perfect manuscript and a properly-sized and prepared cover to use this service unless you are willing to spend a lot of money in fees and proofs until you get it right. There is absolutely no hand holding through the process.

The upside to printing through Lightning Source is that your wholesale costs will be lower than other POD printers, and your book will be available to a vast distribution network of wholesalers, retailers and booksellers—including Amazon and Barnes&Noble.

Espresso Book Machine

The Espresso Book Machine (EBM) (www.ondemandbooks.com) takes print-on-demand a whole step further. They provide equipment to select locations allowing readers to choose a book and have it printed in about fifteen minutes while they wait. You will not find EBMs in every city, at least not yet, and in some states, there are few locations. EBMs offer some exciting possibilities. Think about creating a book with recipes or stories gathered during a family reunion, and being able to deliver the book to family members a few hours later.

Print Production Basics

One of your first major decisions is whether to print the book in color or in black-and-white. The cover, of course, will be in full color since that will not cost you more, and color covers are standard across the industry. Color *interiors*, however, add significantly to the cost. At print-on-demand printers, if you choose a color interior, every page will be considered a color page, even if it only has black-and-white text on it. If the book is in color, it is color throughout. An offset printer may be able to insert color pages either as a section in the middle, or in select places throughout the book. Either way, the cost of full color books is much higher than books with black-and-white interiors.

Consider that you may be able to create a 200 page, (in inches) 8.5 x 11 book in black-and-white for around $7 wholesale, whereas a color version of that same book could run $80 or more. **Tip:** One way to give your family the stories in black-and-white and the photographs in full color is to print the history book with the images in black-and-white, then create a separate companion photo book with the best images. That way, you print the black-and-white book for $7 wholesale, along with a 20 page color photo book for $10 to $15—together, still cheaper than a full-color interior.

Interior Files

All books have interior files and cover files. The interior file will contain everything from the title page to the index, including the images. You will set up your manuscript in the physical size of the final book, called the trim size. The paper will be slightly larger than the final size so it can be trimmed off neatly to give the book a finished look.

The most common trim sizes (in inches) are 6 x 9, 7 x 10 and 8.5 x 11. You can create a book of nearly any size, but if you will use one of these common sizes, the production cost will be lower and your options for printers will be greater.

Choose a trim size based upon how many pages there are in the manuscript, and how large you wish to display the images. When you are ready to create the layout, you should have an idea of whether your book will run 50 pages or 500.

The 6 x 9 or 7 x 10 size is nice if you think the reader will sit down and read the book cover to cover because these books are easy to hold. If the book becomes too thick at one of the above sizes, you may want to increase the page size to 8.5 x 11—the size of a traditional piece of paper in the United States. This size is a little less comfortable to hold while reading, but ideal for a book meant for research, and has more room on each page to display images.

Cover Files

You will not create your cover file until you have chosen the trim size, the binding, and have the manuscript ready because the number of pages will determine the spine width.

Most printers offer the following binding options:

Hardbound also Called Case Bound. Hardbound covers are created from thick cardboard pieces covered in material, glued or sewn to the interior at the spine. You will have the option of a plain cloth cover, wrapping the cloth cover with a dust jacket, or a full-color, glossy paper cover— like a textbook.

Softbound also Called Paperback or Perfect Binding. Softbound covers are created from a thick, paper cover glued to the interior pages at the spine.

Lay-flat. Lay-flat is a more expensive option than softbound, but best for workbooks or cookbooks that need to lay flat to be used easily

Each of the following binding styles are not preferred by librarians because they do not have spines, so the book must be removed from the shelf in order to read the title.

Saddle Stitch. Saddle stitch books are laid out in two page spreads, folded in half, then stapled at the spine. Standard (in inches) 8.5 x 11 paper becomes a 5.5 x 8.5 book, or an 11 x 17 paper becomes an 8.5 x 11 book. The covers are created from thicker card stock and place on the outside of the collated pages before folding and stapling. Saddle stitch is best for books under 48 pages.

Side Stitch. In a side-stitched book, pages are collated, loose card stock covers are placed on the front and back, then stapled on the left-hand side near the edge.

Spiral or Wire-O. These books look like a spiral notebook—the kind you used in school. One problem with spiral or wire-o is that every time the pages are turned, they rub against the binding. Eventually, the pages will tear from the book easily.

For family histories, softbound or hardbound is best. Either looks professional, has a nice spine so you can read the title when the book is on the shelf, and lasts longer than spiral, wire-o, or old-fashioned comb binding which is expensive and does not hold up well over time.

Final Files

Most printers will accept PDF (Portable Document Format) files. Once you have your manuscript looking the way you want it to, save it as a PDF and send it to the printer. More about the mechanics of saving PDF files in Section 2.

Print Distribution Basics

To deliver a printed book to an interested reader, it could be sold through a bookstore—a brick and mortar store or online. You could: distribute them yourself by selling them on your own website; print a bunch and take them to a family reunion; ask interested family members to send orders to you; or, use an online print-on-demand service where buyers could purchase a copy for themselves. These are all easy options for distributing printed books to readers.

Selling books through a brick and mortar store is a little more complicated. Most bookstores order directly through one of the major wholesalers—Ingram (Lightning Source) or Baker&Taylor. To sell books to a chain bookstore, you must have an account with one or both of the major wholesalers. For a family history, however, chances are that the trouble you will go through to get an account will not be worth it.

There are exceptions. If you have someone famous in your family, or if you have the kind of story with widespread public interest, then traditional bookstore distribution channels may be an option for you.

Another exception is selling through a local independent bookstore. A local store owner may be willing to stock a few books bought directly from you, but expect this to be the exception rather than the rule. You may have more luck with a local museum shop where making small purchases from local authors is more common. Museum stores will purchase a few copies at a time, so give them an easy way to re-order.

Be aware of the expectations of book sellers. Wholesalers will expect you to give them up to a 50 percent discount, so they can make a few dollars and allow the end seller (the bookstore) to make a few dollars on the sale as well. You can probably offer a smaller discount to a local bookstore or museum shop, more like 20 to 30 percent if you are not using a wholesaler.

Then there is the matter of returns. Bookstores and wholesalers expect to be able to return books if they go unsold. This can be an accounting hassle for you, not to mention that they may send the book back years later, in no condition to re-sell, but expect credit for the return anyway. For small publishers, the only way around this is to sell books on a *non-returnable* basis. You may have to offer a bigger discount to induce the bookstore or museum shop to a non-returnable sale, but the greater discount is almost always worth not dealing with returns.

Electronic Publishing

Except for adult fiction, printed books still hold about ninety percent of the book market. However, people are reading more and more via dedicated eReaders and on other electronic devices such as tablets. On tablets, readers use an application (app) to display the book as the dedicated eReaders do. As smart phones, tablets and other mobile devices become more widely used in schools and in offices, electronic books will become even more popular. Electronic books are cheaper, mobile and easier to store.

Currently, there are three primary formats for electronic publishing—PDF, MOBI and EPUB.

PDF (Portable Document Format)

Creating a PDF does not require a publisher or a distributor. PDF is a file type developed by the Adobe Corporation that solved cross-platform problems between users' computers. Before the PDF, sending a file to a person using a different operating system (PC or Mac) or software (Word or Word Perfect) meant that the recipient could not open or read the document.

You can convert almost any type of file to a PDF and almost every computer comes with the free Adobe Acrobat Reader pre-installed. Download it free from

Adobe (www.adobe.com). PDFs can be opened and read on most electronic devices including tablets.

One upside to PDFs is the ease of creation. Most word processing and page layout software will save their files to PDFs. Another is that saving to PDF keeps the page formatting exactly as you designed it. Everything will stay in place—the text, the pictures, and the captions.

One downside to PDFs is that when the reader closes the file, their place is lost. Each time they open the book, they will have to page down to where they left off.

Another downside is that documents designed using (in inches) 8.5 x 11 pages are read easily on a computer screen or iPad, but may be almost impossible to read on a smaller device such as a mini-tablet or a phone, because the pages are a fixed size, more like viewing a photograph than reading a text document. A better option for smaller devices is to use a format that allows the text to re-flow, such as MOBI or EPUB.

MOBI and EPUB

Where electronic publishing gets a little more complicated is in the creation and distribution of different formats for different devices. There are two primary formats for eReaders or apps that imitate eReaders—Kindle's proprietary format MOBI, and the EPUB format used by many other devices. Acting as your own publisher for these formats is not impossible, but not simple either.

Publishing for Kindle

The Kindle is Amazon's dedicated eReader. To publish for Kindle, use the Kindle Direct Publishing (KDP) service (kdp.amazon.com). You will be able to upload a Word document or a PDF, and Amazon will convert it to their proprietary MOBI format. Amazon will handle all sales and distribution. Readers will make their purchase through Amazon and download the book to their Kindle or a device with a Kindle app.

Amazon pays you a royalty based upon the book's retail price. In 2014, any book with a retail price under $9.99 will generate a 70 percent royalty, whereas books priced at $10.00 or higher receive a 30 percent royalty.

One nice feature of Kindle books is their ability to sync across devices, meaning that readers can switch from their Kindle to their tablet or smart phone and sync the files to maintain their place in the book.

Publishing for Other eReaders

While most word processing software will create a PDF, you may need special software to create an EPUB file. Since so many devices are using this format, it may become easier to create an EPUB in the future. If you have a Mac, Pages software will create EPUB files. Adobe InDesign will create an EPUB file on a PC, but the software is expensive. Microsoft Word will allow you to save your manuscript as an HTML file and then you can use the free Calibre software (calibre-ebook.com) to convert an HTML file into an EPUB.

If you create your own EPUB files, download Adobe's free Digital Editions software (www.adobe.com). Use Calibre to preview how the book looks before sending it to readers or elsewhere for distribution.

Electronic Production Basics

Electronic books, like printed books, need an interior file and a cover file but there are differences in how the files must be prepared—sometimes big differences.

Interior Files as PDFs

Setting up your manuscript for a PDF is almost the same as setting it up for print production. You can set it up as two-page spreads, so that the reader experiences the book the same way they would if they were reading a printed version, or you can set it up as a single page document without right-hand or left-hand pages. This allows the reader to keep a single page on the screen which will make it easier to read on a device such as an iPad.

You can use a word processor or page layout program to create your PDF file, or you can use a presentation program such as PowerPoint or Keynote for the Mac. Word processors have the best spell and grammar checkers, but presentation programs may give you greater control over combining text and images. The slide sorter view, for example, lets you move information around much easier than cutting and pasting in your word processor. Page layout programs (albeit the most expensive software option) will give you the greatest control over both text and images.

Interior Files as MOBIs or EPUBs

Preparing a manuscript for conversion to MOBI or EPUB is, in some respects, easier than laying out and formatting a PDF for electronic or print production. Electronic books must be simple, and without a lot of complicated formatting because the look of an electronic book is controlled largely by the reader. The reader is able to adjust the type size to suit their needs so the text must re-flow within the eReader's window.

While it is possible for you to create a MOBI or EPUB file yourself, it may be easier to let an eBook aggregator or distributor create the file for you so that there are no glitches when the file is read by electronic devices.

Cover Files

While it is not necessary to include a cover file with your electronic book, many eReaders will show the cover in the catalog on the device, and most eBook outlets will show a thumbnail of the cover in their catalogs for sale. Make sure your title is readable in the small thumbnail.

Electronic Distribution Basics

How an electronic book is distributed largely depends upon the format.

Distributing PDFs

Distributing a PDF is simple. You can send it directly to the reader in an email. Fortunately, PDF files can be optimized which makes the file small enough to send even long manuscripts with photographs and illustrations by email.

Another option is to post your PDF online for readers to download for themselves. You could send interested readers a link, or they could use a search engine to discover it. You could also create a website and post your PDF behind a password so that only paying customers can access it.

One downside to *selling* your book as a PDF, however, is limiting distribution to paying customers. There are tools that allow you to mark copies with the name of the original buyer so if the book is widely shared, you will know who made it available. Other tools allow you to lock the PDF from printing or to password protect the file. Practically, however, once you distribute your book in a PDF format, it may be re-distributed without your knowledge.

Distribution for the Kindle

The distribution of Kindle books is done through Amazon and you can publish your eBook directly through their distributor CreateSpace (that also handles printed books) (www.createspace.com), or Kindle Direct Publishing (kdp.amazon.com), if you plan to publish only in the Kindle format. Right now, Kindle holds a majority of the eBook market through either its dedicated reader or through the Kindle app available for tablets or smart phones.

Distribution for Devices Using the EPUB Format

The EPUB format is used by hundreds of different devices. If you are able to create an EPUB file, you can distribute the book yourself, much the same way as you would a PDF file (above). There are also hundreds of distribution outlets for EPUB books including iTunes (www.itunes.com), the Android App Store (play.google.com), Google Books (books.google.com), Kobo (www.kokobooks.com), Smashwords (www.smashwords.com), and Gumroad (www.gumroad.com), to name a few. These online bookstores sell electronic books, acting as a wholesaler between you and the end user.

Rather than dealing with hundreds of online bookstores, consider using an aggregator. Aggregators charge a fee, but they will prepare your manuscript for distribution across multiple platforms making sure the file passes the standards tests for different devices. They will also prepare the file for the many apps (applications) that mimic eReaders such as the Nook app or the Kindle app.

Aggregators will handle sales through the different electronic book outlets, take a percentage as their sales commission and pay the rest to you as a royalty.

The following are all eBook aggregators: First Edition Design Publishing (www.firsteditiondesignpublishing.com), Bookwire (www.bookwire.com), Ingram (www.ingramcontent.com), INscribe (inscribedigital.com), Smashwords (www.smashwords.com), and BookBaby (www.bookbaby.com).

Distribution of Other Electronic Files

Services such as Gumroad (gumroad.com), allow you to upload your electronic file(s) to their servers. Gumroad accepts audio, video or zipped bundles, if you have more than one book available or want to include an audio file along with your book file. To sell your book, place a link on your website taking viewers to Gumroad to buy it. You price your book, Gumroad keeps a percentage as a hosting and processing fee, they pay you the rest. In essence, Gumroad is taking care of the credit card processing and electronic delivery. Once the item is paid for, the buyer will receive a download link.

Distribution to Groups

If you want to sell a quantity of books to an organization, for example, you can use Amazon's Whispercast service (whispercast.amazon.com). The organization will create an account and send an invitation URL to its members. If the member accepts the invitation, the organization buys a copy for that person. After the member receives the book, Amazon charges the organization's credit card for the sale. This would work for a family reunion, for example, by pre-selling books during the reunion, setting up a bank account with a debit card on behalf of the reunion and using the funds collected to pay for the books through Whispercast.

Global Distribution

One of the biggest advantages to publishing electronically through one of the major distributors such as Amazon's Kindle Direct Publishing (kdp.amazon.com), or Barnes&Noble's Nook Press (nookpress.com), is that they will make your eBook available to people across the globe. There is no negotiating of foreign rights or dealing with a foreign publisher to distribute the book on another continent. If you have family members across the world, publishing electronically may be a good option for you.

Distribution by Gift Card

Enthrill Books (enthrillbooks.com), enables you to use a pre-activated gift card allowing the recipient to download your book either in the EPUB or MOBI format. You could take the pre-activated cards to a family reunion, for example, to sell or give away to your family members.

Distribution to Libraries

One final consideration is placing your book with the major genealogical collections across the country and into the local libraries where your family once resided. While most libraries still focus on print books, they are coming around to the idea of purchasing licensing rights for eBooks. Most of the time, family histories or genealogies are kept in non-circulating collections, so the electronic format would allow the book to be lent. OverDrive (www.overdrive.com), is one of the leading digital distributors of electronic books to libraries, schools and some retail outlets. If you are interested in selling your eBook to libraries, check out the publisher services on their website.

Online Publishing

For those of you who may want to make your book widely available and are not interested in selling it, publishing online may be a good option. There are a couple of ways to do so. You can use an online book publisher (Google Books), or you can act as your own publisher by using online publishing tools such as blogging software, website builders, social media or on a genealogical website featuring family trees.

The difference between an online book and an electronic book is how it is delivered. Online books and electronic books are both in an electronic format. An online book stays on a server somewhere where readers can use a web browser to access the book via the Internet. An electronic book is more likely to be distributed to a reading device such as a Kindle, Nook or smart phone.

The upside to publishing online is that anyone with Internet access can find and read your book. Many of the options below cost nothing to set up and use, although, you are completely at the mercy of the host as to whether your site stays up or whether the company folds and your free site folds with it. Another option is to pay for your own website which will give you more options for the look and feel of the material or whether you want to sell the book rather than give it away. But, you must continue paying the hosting fee or the site will come down and your book with it.

The following are options for publishing a book online:

Online Book Publishers

Google Books is one of the only online book publishers I have found to date, meaning that they sell books meant to be read via the Internet using a web browser. Google Books uses a proprietary format allowing readers to choose between PDFs formatted exactly as the publisher formatted the book, read through a browser platform that presents the book in side-by-side pages as if reading a printed book. Google's browser-based software also gives readers the option of reading the book like other dedicated eReaders. The reader can change the type size or the font and the book text will re-flow. If you want to publish a book through Google Books, sign up through their Google Play Books Partner Center (play.google.com/books/publish/).

Amazon offers something similar allowing readers to purchase a book for their Kindle, also allowing them to access the book from a web browser through the Kindle Cloudreader software (read.kindle.com). The experience of reading a Kindle book online is similar to reading from the Kindle device itself.

Publishing a Book by Blog

Blog is short for web log. Blogging software allows publishers to post new content easily and quickly. If you can use email, you can blog. The process is similar. You will use a headline to alert the reader, and the body text to tell the story and display images. The difficulty of publishing a book on a blog is organizing in a way that the reader understands what to read in what order, and keeping the segments short enough to avoid scrolling and scrolling and scrolling. (See Chapter 17: Converting a Print Manuscript to a Blog.)

Publishing a Book Using Social Media

Facebook (www.facebook.com), is the most popular social media site right now, although it has not always been, and may not be in the future. The appeal of Facebook is that it is so easy to connect with other people (family members) interested in reading your material. The downside of using something like Facebook to deliver your book's content is that each post can be only so long, shorter, even than blog posts. You will be delivering your book in little dribs and drabs. Facebook may be a better place to obtain additional stories from family members while you are writing, more so than playing host to your finished book. (See Chapter 18: Converting a Print Manuscript for Social Media.)

Publishing a Book on Your Own Website

If you create your own website to publish your book, you can install blogging software such as WordPress, use a dedicated online genealogy program such as The Next Generation (TNG) (lythgoes.net/genealogy/software.php), or more traditional HTML coding using any number of HTML editors (website building software) such as Adobe Dreamweaver (www.adobe.com).

If you use web-based genealogy software such as The Next Generation (TNG), you may have trouble publishing your stories as a book *per se*, because the software is not meant for book publishing, it displays family trees, photographs and source information as a website. TNG offers "featured articles" that can hold large volumes of text as well as a "histories" feature for short stories linked to individuals within your tree.

If you create your own website and use an HTML editor, you will have complete control over how the site looks, and how your book will be organized as web pages. (See Chapter 16: Converting a Print Manuscript to a Website.)

Publishing a Book with a Genealogy Service

Neither the paid genealogy services Ancestry (www.ancestry.com), or MyHeritage (www.myheritage.com), nor the free service FamilySearch (www.familysearch.org) (or any of the other genealogy-based search sites) were designed as book publishing platforms; although, many offer tools to attach stories and photographs to individuals within an online family tree. Publishing your book in this way is similar to publishing on a social media site—short snippets rather than a beginning-to-end book.

Note: FamilySearch, Ancestry and MyHeritage have book or booklet publishing options that use your online tree to create printed books. When investigating the process, I found that the cost was quite a bit higher than using a print-on-demand printer, and the options for what to include or exclude was a bit clumsy, at least at this point. If you are going to create a print version of your research, it is worth the effort to use a dedicated book printer.

Online Production Basics

If you publish online, preparing your manuscript is relatively easy. Although, how you prepare it depends upon where you are going to place it on the Internet. Let us start with Google Books since they are the exception to the rule, and then we will look into making your book into blog posts or web pages.

Files for Google Books

If you publish online through Google Books, you can upload both a PDF version and an EPUB version, so the reader can choose whether to view the book exactly as you have it laid out, or as flowing text they can control through Google's browser-based platform. PDF and EPUB are the only two file formats Google Books accepts for upload. They will also accept a printed book and scan it for you, making it possible to create a new eBook out of an older, out-of-print title.

Thumbnail-sized cover files are used on Google Books in their online catalog.

Files for Blog Posts

While you can organize your material as a complete book on a blog, you must organize in a way that lets readers know how to follow the stories one after the other, and split the manuscript into short segments (posts) to keep scrolling to a minimum.

Each post requires a headline and body text, similar to composing an email. Blog posts can include images and captions. You can also add keywords to categorize each post so that readers can find the blog using a search engine.

Readers familiar with feed reader programs can subscribe to your blog so that they are notified every time you create a new post.

You can use your cover image as a part of the blog's header so that it is always visible no matter which post the reader is viewing.

Files for Social Media

Publishing to a social media site is similar to publishing to a blog. Posting to a blog or social media keeps your short snippets in one place with the latest post at the top. The older posts will move down as the new posts appear.

On social media, if you create a page (sometimes called fan page) dedicated to your book, readers can come to that page to see everything you have posted, similar to visiting a blog, but if readers are "following" your page (have "liked" it), then the snippets will be delivered to the reader through the newsfeed on their own pages.

For each post, use the headline to catch the viewer's attention as they skim their newsfeed (the posts coming in). Place the text in the body, and add images. Some social media platforms allow you to caption each image, and "tag" the people in the image. Tagging is like adding a keyword to the image. It helps people find the image using the search feature on the social media site, or by using a search engine.

Use your cover image in the header area of the book's page, or as the profile image so that every time you post, the book's cover is shown in the little icon next to the post. Facebook uses square profile images and book covers are longer than they are wide, so you may have to add a bit of white space on either side of your cover image to make it square. Otherwise it could be cut off at the top and bottom when displayed.

Files for a Website

Creating your own website gives you a lot of flexibility for how and what you make available to readers.

Web pages can hold text, images, video or audio files and contain links to other resources on the Internet. To publish your book as a website, use an HTML editor to create a page for each story or chapter and navigation links to help the reader move from story to story logically.

Keywords are used on web pages the same way they are used on blog posts to help the search engines find the web page. HTML editing software and most website building tools online offer a way to include keywords in the metadata for each page.

Use your cover image in the the website's header, or alongside the text on the home page.

Files for a Genealogy Service

Most genealogical websites where you can build an online family tree have a way to attach stories to individuals or groups.

Ancestry provides two ways to attach stories to people in your family tree. One method is to use the story view settings. Ancestry uses the documents you have linked to the person to suggest a storyline, and gives you the option of adding text and photographs to the story view page. Another option is to add stories directly through the media gallery section where you can also add images, video or audio.

The process is similar on FamilySearch. You will add stories in the "memories" section of your family tree where you can also add a picture.

At MyHeritage, each individual in your tree has a page where you can add information and media files such as photographs or links to video files.

Cover files are a little more difficult to place at one of these online options, unless you want a cover image attached to an individual.

Copy and Paste Text Cleanly

The easiest way to prepare text for any online option, is to copy and paste from your word processor. However, many word processors add code for formatting features such as margins, fonts, font size, bold or italics. These codes do not always translate cleanly to email, blog posts or websites. Word processors use an 8-bit environment for formatting, while many of the tools of the Internet use a 7-bit environment which can cause conflicts. What you can end up with is unexpected characters in your text, mostly where you expect punctuation to be.

This, for example, is a quote copied from a Word document into an email:
From Word: "Jacob's intended return ..."
Copied into email: "Jacob@s intended return ..."

One way to avoid these unexpected ASCII characters is to copy the text into a plain text editing program such as Notepad first. Notepad will remove all formatting, leaving a plain text (.txt) version of whatever you are copying and pasting. The plain text version can then be used in an email, a blog post or a website without any unexpected characters surfacing.

Create Web-Friendly File Names

Tools of the Internet also prefer standard file-names. So, file names that are acceptable on your local computer may contain unexpected characters when posted online. For example:
Local file: Jacob Wilson's will.pdf
Online becomes: Jacob%20Wilson%20s%20Will.pdf (depending upon the server settings)

For clean file names, avoid punctuation except for periods and use underscores for spaces. Either of these file names would be fine, for example:
Jacob.Wilson.Will.pdf
Jacob_Wilson_Will.pdf

Online Distribution Basics

If you publish online, you have largely determined how the book will be distributed to the reader—on a blog, a website or within a social media platform. You do not have to distribute it, the readers will come to the book. You need only take the steps necessary to help readers find the book online—good, descriptive keywords, great content and a willingness to get the word out.

What is the easiest way to prepare a book to distribute to family members at the least cost? That would be a PDF. As long as the PDF is designed for easy reading on the screen, the book can be distributed by email. For some family members, a PDF is perfect. If they are used to reading on screen or on a large format tablet such as an iPad, they will appreciate the PDF. For other family members, print will always be preferred.

What, then, is the easiest way to prepare a book for sale? The easiest way is to create an eBook and use an eBook aggregator to convert it to the different electronic formats for you. The aggregator will also submit the files to the various sales outlets online, collect the sales price minus the online bookstore's fee, and pay you a royalty from the sale. Creating an eBook is simpler than creating a book for print because there are a few simple formatting and image placement rules to follow. The reader is able to change the font or type size to suit his or her needs, so the formatting must remain fluid. There is a fee to have an eBook aggregator prepare and submit your manuscript, but for those family members who are used to a dedicated eReader, this option will delight them.

Publishing a book online and in print are a bit more challenging than publishing PDFs and eBooks.

Publishing online has organizational challenges but many options are without cost. Online publishing has the risk of all other electronic products—obsolescence. If the company hosting your website folds, the social media site becomes unpopular, or your blog is lost in a server crash, the book is lost.

The best, most permanent way to preserve your research and writing is to publish in print. A printed book will be appreciated by your family members. A book printed today, given the technology and materials, should last one hundred years or more. If preserved well, a modern book will last much longer. In the event of natural or personal disaster, giving a few copies of your book to the major genealogical libraries around the country will preserve your research and writing for generations to come.

You do not have to publish exclusively in print, however. Sections Three and Four contain advice for converting your print manuscript to an electronic or online book easily.

Chapter 5

Right Tool for the Right Job

To make your way from idea to finished book, using the right tool for the right job will save you time and frustration.

In a perfect world, you would use an organizational tool to set up the table of contents and organize your notes, a word processor to draft your manuscript, an image capture program to scan documents and other printed materials, an image editor to crop, size and alter images, a page layout program to typeset the book so that it reads and looks its best, and backup tools to keep your manuscript and image files safe from disaster.

In general, organizational tools are not the best place to format text correctly, word processors are not the best place to lay out book pages, and page layout programs are not the best word processors.

Realistically, you may not want to invest your time and money in all of this software. You may not need to. What you do_need is an understanding of the rules of readability for books; and either, the willingness to learn how to create a layout, typeset the text, and prepare images in the software you already own, or the recognition that the software you have will not do the job well. If the latter is the case, you can engage professional help or invest in software more suited to the job.

Organizing

In the preliminary stages, you may want software to keep you organized. Scrivener (www.literatureandlatte.com/scrivener.php) is a powerful organizing tool to gather your notes, pictures, video clips, or thoughts. It is available for both PC and Mac.

If you use an outline, one panel shows your outline in a menu that you can use to rearrange files, and expand or collapse depending upon what you want to see while you are working. You can split files into pieces to create a detailed outline.

If you are more visual, you can see your notes organized on a cork board. If you want to keep your sources attached to each note, you can do so either in the body of the text or off to the side in a panel designed to document sources.

At any time, you can move notes from one place to another using the drag and drop features in the cork board or outline, helping to organize your information into a cohesive whole.

Similar organizing software includes: Microsoft OneNote (www.onenote.com), and Evernote (www.evernote.com). Both of these organizing tools have the advantage of being available on your desktop and by app on mobile devices with the ability to sync files. I use these apps to add notes or ideas when I am out and about, but when I am in the office writing, I use Scrivener to organize.

Word Processing

At some point, move your notes from an organizing tool into a word processor. Whether you are at the stage to add formatting or you are still writing and want to collect your material chapter by chapter, a word processor is a better tool than organizing software to create a complete manuscript.

Word processing programs are best for editing because you can review changes before they become final.

Word processors are ideal for creating eBooks. Unfortunately, most word processing software falls short when creating layouts and correct typesetting for print books because they lack the sophistication to create the best-looking pages.

Word processors often hyphenate incorrectly or add space between words to avoid hyphenating which can create rivers of white or blank areas through the type. Word processors do not have nearly the kind of control over how tight or how loose text is typeset which also can result in dense or dark areas of text on the page. Most word processors do not have as much control over margins, columns and text wrap around images as page layout programs do.

Unfortunately, page layout software can be expensive, so you may opt to layout and typeset your final manuscript in your word processing software. If you do, be prepared to learn about the advanced features. Fortunately, some word processors have helpful time-saving features to automatically create a table of contents, an index and footnotes, for example.

There are numerous word processing programs available including: Microsoft Word (office.microsoft.com), Pages for Mac (www.apple.com), WordPerfect (www.wordperfect.com), OpenOffice Writer (www.openoffice.org), LibreOffice (www.libreoffice.org) and Google Docs (docs.google.com).

Microsoft Word has become the standard among book designers and packagers, professional editors, some eBook aggregators, and online resellers. For book designers and book packagers, Word files can be imported directly into more sophisticated page layout software without much trouble. For editors, Word has a "Track Changes" feature that allows you to see and accept or reject an editor's changes. Most eBook aggregators prefer Word files because they can convert the file for the requirements of the different eBook readers easily. And, some online resellers will accept Word files from which to create print and electronic books.

Page Layout

When typesetting print books, you will achieve the best results from a page layout program. The two major powerhouses are: Adobe InDesign (www.adobe.com), and QuarkXPress (www.quark.com). Pages for Mac (www.apple.com), was designed as a word processor, but has many of the same features as the best page layout programs.

Page layout programs are designed to put the finishing touches on book-length manuscripts using the same tools professional typesetters use. These programs also have the ability to handle full-color books and, for the time being, are best for converting word-processed text into good looking eBooks in the EPUB format used by many eReaders.

PDF is another popular electronic format, and page layout programs create beautiful PDFs with the appropriate file sizes and quality for printing, emailing or posting online.

The biggest advantage to using a page layout program is the control you have over where items are placed on the page in relationship to other items, the ability to create precise text formatting styles (rules) for different needs, and the flexible layouts possible with master pages that create grids for different page styles.

The sophistication of these programs is a big step up from even the best word processors. Unfortunately, most page layout programs come with both a hefty price tag and a hefty learning curve. For some, using a book designer or packager to take your final manuscript from as good as a word processor can do, to as good as a New York publisher could do, may be a better tradeoff than buying and learning a page layout program.

Image Capture

There are two ways to turn a printed photograph or document into a digital image—you can photograph it or you can scan it. For items such as photographs pasted into a scrapbook, heirloom objects or photographs with textured surfaces, re-photographing the item may give you the best results.

For most flat items, however, scanning will give you a good digital image. Producing a good, print-ready scan will save you time and effort later.

There is more information about scanning in Chapter 8: Images for Print.

Image Editing

The best way to prepare images in the correct physical size and resolution is to use an image editing program.

There are hundreds of image editors, including online tools, free downloads, apps for mobile devices, pre-installed software, and those designed for professional photographers. One of the best is Adobe Photoshop. For most people, the consumer version called Photoshop Elements (www.adobe.com), will do everything you need to complete your book project.

Illustration

While it is possible to create a book cover in a word processor or a page layout program, to create the best-looking images and type, you may want to use illustration software, also called vector editing programs. The most popular among graphic designers is Adobe Illustrator (www.adobe.com).

There are many others available, including: CorelDraw Graphics Suite (www.coreldraw.com), Xara Designer Pro (www.xara.com), and Inkscape (www.inkscape.org). This is another case where the cost of buying the program (and learning it) may be better spent hiring a cover designer.

Utilities and Backup

While you are writing, make backups—frequently. You never know when your hard drive will crash or some other calamity may come your way. One way to create on-going backups is to use one of the cloud services such as Carbonite (www.carbonite.com), MyPCBackup (www.mypcbackup.com), Mozy (www.mozy.com) or SugarSync (www.sygarsync.com). If you keep good backups and something happens, you can always retrieve the most-recent backup of your manuscript once you are up and running again.

If you also want to share files, use a file sharing service such as Dropbox (www.dropbox.com), Hightail (formerly YouSendIt) (www.hightail.com), Box.com (www.box.com), Google Drive (drive.google.com) or Microsoft OneDrive (onedrive.live.com).

These services are perfect for sharing copies of your manuscript, even if the file is large. *Do not keep your only copy* on one of these services, however, because anyone who shares the folder with you has the power to delete it.

The most secure place to keep backups is in the cloud, or on a portable hard drive, stored away from your home in a safe deposit box.

How many or how few of these tools you utilize is up to you. You may find that the right tool for the right job is easiest. Or, you may prefer hiring someone to handle the tasks you would rather not tackle. Thankfully, most family histories are completed without spending a king's ransom on software or professional help.

SECTION 2

The goal in this section on print publishing is for you to learn how to produce a book that looks as good and reads as easily as any book from a traditional publisher.

There is not enough space in this book to give instructions for formatting using each of the major word processing or page layout programs. The terminology used in this section, however, should give you what you need to use the help features in your software to accomplish each task.

Chapter 6

Page Layout for Print

The most important element in laying out a page for print is to make the page easy to read. The best way to do that is to follow the long-established rules of readability. Desktop publishing offers many options for innovative ways to create columns, employ fonts, and place illustrations—too many perhaps. Leave the wild innovating to the graphic designers on magazine staffs. The tried and true rules for book design are still the best.

A poorly or unusually designed book may make your readers skeptical of the quality of the information. Too much work goes into researching your family and writing a book to have that effort spoiled by poor design, when good design is so easy to accomplish. Your book will look its best and be easiest to read if you stick to the tried and true rules for book design.

Page Size

How much real estate you have to work with depends upon the trim size of the page. The trim size is the finished size of the book. Choosing a trim size pits look against cost. A 12" x 12" coffee table book is fabulous to look at, but a 6" x 9" book is much easier to sit and read.

An offset printer can create books in just about any size, but you must order a minimum number of books to make the price per book worth it. If the cost of setup for a run of specially-sized books is $500 and the print-per-book charge is $20, if you only order 10 books, the cost per book would be $70 ($50 + $20).

You will save money if you choose one of the common page sizes offered by print-on-demand printers. Most print-on-demand printers do not charge a fee for setup, they only charge to produce each book—and they can produce books one at a time. The most common page sizes for print-on-demand printers are (in inches) 6 x 9, 7 x 10 and 8.5 x 11.

No matter what page size you choose, the rules for good layout are essentially the same. The one small exception is that the larger the page, the larger proportionally the elements such as fonts, white space and images should be.

Page Count

Book interiors must be multiples of two (front and back of a single sheet). If you use an offset printer, they may require page counts in signatures of 4, 8, 16, 32, 48, 64 or even 80. Offset printers print use paper on rolls many feet wide and when the paper is folded and cut, it will form a signature of one of the multiples of four (4).

Signatures can be an issue if, for example, you have written a one hundred page book, but the printer's signature requirement is eighty pages. In that case, you would have to reduce your book by twenty pages, or increase it by sixty pages in order to meet the signature requirement. Otherwise, you would have sixty blank pages at the end of your one hundred page book.

Luckily, print-on-demand printers use simple two page signatures—front and back.

Blank Pages

By publishing tradition, chapters and most front matter and back matter elements, should begin on a right-hand page. You may have blank pages if a chapter runs an odd number of pages because the last page will be blank so that the next section can start on a right-hand page.

If you have blank pages, they should be completely blank—no headers and no page numbers.

White Space

The biggest misconception about laying out a book is that you must economize the space by cramming as much as you can onto a single page. Please do not. The reader needs a break from solid text either from the margins around the edges, the space between columns, paragraphs, words, and letters, or all of the above.

Altering the spacing between the letters (tracking) and the space between the lines of text (leading) can make the page look more or less dense. If you want to make the page look a little less dense or dark, use a book font such as Bookman because it is wider and more open, rather than a newspaper font such as Times which is thin and meant to be read in narrow newspaper columns. By increasing the space between the lines of text (leading) or between the paragraphs, the page will look less dense. In the example, the page on the left looks dense. The one on the right is much more open.

Lorem ipsum dolor sit amet, consectetur adipisicing elit, sed do eiusmod tempor incididunt ut labore et dolore magna aliqua. Ut enim ad minim veniam, quis nostrud exercitation ullamco laboris nisi ut aliquip ex ea commodo consequat. Duis aute irure dolor in reprehenderit in voluptate velit esse cillum dolore eu fugiat nulla pariatur. Excepteur sint occaecat cupidatat non proident, sunt in culpa qui officia deserunt mollit anim id est laborum.

Lorem ipsum dolor sit amet, consectetur adipisicing elit, sed do eiusmod tempor incididunt ut labore et dolore magna aliqua. Ut enim ad minim veniam, quis nostrud exercitation ullamco laboris nisi ut aliquip ex ea commodo consequat. Duis aute irure dolor in reprehenderit in voluptate velit esse cillum dolore eu fugiat nulla pariatur. Excepteur sint occaecat cupidatat non proident, sunt in culpa qui officia deserunt mollit anim id est laborum.

Lorem ipsum dolor sit amet, consectetur adipisicing elit, sed do eiusmod tempor incididunt ut labore et dolore magna aliqua. Ut enim ad minim veniam, quis nostrud exercitation ullamco laboris nisi ut aliquip ex ea commodo consequat. Duis aute irure dolor in reprehenderit in voluptate velit esse cillum dolore eu fugiat nulla pariatur. Excepteur sint occaecat cupidatat non proident, sunt in culpa qui officia deserunt mollit anim id est laborum.

Lorem ipsum dolor sit amet, consectetur adipisicing elit, sed do eiusmod tempor incididunt ut labore et dolore magna aliqua. Ut enim ad minim veniam, quis nostrud exercitation ullamco laboris nisi ut aliquip ex ea commodo consequat. Duis aute irure dolor in reprehenderit in voluptate velit esse cillum dolore eu fugiat nulla pariatur. Excepteur sint occaecat cupidatat non proident, sunt in culpa qui officia deserunt mollit anim id est laborum.

Lorem ipsum dolor sit amet, consectetur adipisicing elit, sed do eiusmod tempor incididunt ut labore et dolore magna aliqua. Ut

Lorem ipsum dolor sit amet, consectetur adipisicing elit, sed do eiusmod tempor incididunt ut labore et dolore magna aliqua. Ut enim ad minim veniam, quis nostrud exercitation ullamco laboris nisi ut aliquip ex ea commodo consequat. Duis aute irure dolor in reprehenderit in voluptate velit esse cillum dolore eu fugiat nulla pariatur. Excepteur sint occaecat cupidatat non proident, sunt in culpa qui officia deserunt mollit anim id est laborum.

Lorem ipsum dolor sit amet, consectetur adipisicing elit, sed do eiusmod tempor incididunt ut labore et dolore magna aliqua. Ut enim ad minim veniam, quis nostrud exercitation ullamco laboris nisi ut aliquip ex ea commodo consequat. Duis aute irure dolor in reprehenderit in voluptate velit esse cillum dolore eu fugiat nulla pariatur. Excepteur sint occaecat cupidatat non proident, sunt in culpa qui officia deserunt mollit anim id est laborum.

Lorem ipsum dolor sit amet, consectetur adipisicing elit, sed do eiusmod tempor incididunt ut labore et dolore magna aliqua. Ut enim ad minim veniam, quis nostrud exercitation ullamco laboris nisi ut aliquip ex ea commodo consequat. Duis aute irure dolor in reprehenderit in voluptate velit esse cillum dolore eu fugiat nulla pariatur. Excepteur sint occaecat cupidatat non proident, sunt in culpa qui officia deserunt mollit anim id est laborum.

Lorem ipsum dolor sit amet, consectetur adipisicing elit, sed do eiusmod tempor incididunt ut labore et dolore magna aliqua. Ut enim ad minim veniam, quis nostrud exercitation ullamco laboris nisi ut aliquip ex ea commodo consequat. Duis aute irure dolor in reprehenderit in voluptate velit esse cillum dolore eu fugiat nulla

Dense page (left); Less dense (right).

While giving the page white space, you must also follow the rules governing proximity. Proximity means that objects that belong together should be closer to each other. A caption for a photograph, for example, should be closer to the bottom of the photograph than the next line of text.

Even spacing, between paragraphs or between subheads and paragraphs, is a red flag that the person who designed the layout has little experience. It is easiest in a word processing program to use double returns to separate paragraphs, or to put extra space between a paragraph and the next headline or subhead. Easiest, yes. Most attractive, no. Use styles to create additional space either above or below paragraphs, headlines or subheads without using an extra return. A headline or a subhead should be closer to the text below it than the paragraph above it. In the example on the next page, the type on the left has even spacing. The type on the right has correct spacing.

Page Spreads

Books are laid out in spreads (pages side by side), not individual pages. When a reader opens a book, they see page spreads as a single visual unit. Because of the binding in the center, right and left pages are laid out differently. The rules for what goes on each side of the page spread follows shortly.

Lorem ipsum dolor sit amet, consectetur adipisicing elit, sed do eiusmod tempor incididunt ut labore et dolore magna aliqua. Ut enim ad minim veniam, quis nostrud exercitation ullamco laboris nisi ut aliquip ex ea commodo consequat. Duis aute irure dolor in reprehenderit in voluptate velit esse cillum dolore eu fugiat nulla pariatur. Excepteur sint occaecat cupidatat non proident, sunt in culpa qui officia deserunt mollit anim id est laborum.

Headline Headline Headline

Lorem ipsum dolor sit amet, consectetur adipisicing elit, sed do eiusmod tempor incididunt ut labore et dolore magna aliqua. Ut enim ad minim veniam, quis nostrud exercitation ullamco laboris nisi ut aliquip ex ea commodo consequat. Duis aute irure dolor in reprehenderit in voluptate velit esse cillum dolore eu fugiat nulla pariatur. Excepteur sint occaecat cupidatat non proident, sunt in culpa qui officia deserunt mollit anim id est laborum.

Headline Headline Headline

Lorem ipsum dolor sit amet, consectetur adipisicing elit, sed do eiusmod tempor incididunt ut labore et dolore magna aliqua. Ut enim ad minim veniam, quis nostrud exercitation ullamco laboris nisi ut aliquip ex ea commodo consequat. Duis aute irure dolor in reprehenderit in voluptate velit esse cillum dolore eu fugiat nulla pariatur. Excepteur sint occaecat cupidatat non proident, sunt in culpa qui officia deserunt mollit anim id est laborum.
Lorem ipsum dolor sit amet, consectetur adipisicing elit, sed do eiusmod tempor incididunt ut labore et dolore magna aliqua. Ut enim ad minim veniam, quis nostrud exercitation ullamco laboris

Lorem ipsum dolor sit amet, consectetur adipisicing elit, sed do eiusmod tempor incididunt ut labore et dolore magna aliqua. Ut enim ad minim veniam, quis nostrud exercitation ullamco laboris nisi ut aliquip ex ea commodo consequat. Duis aute irure dolor in reprehenderit in voluptate velit esse cillum dolore eu fugiat nulla pariatur. Excepteur sint occaecat cupidatat non proident, sunt in culpa qui officia deserunt mollit anim id est laborum.

Headline Headline Headline
Lorem ipsum dolor sit amet, consectetur adipisicing elit, sed do eiusmod tempor incididunt ut labore et dolore magna aliqua. Ut enim ad minim veniam, quis nostrud exercitation ullamco laboris nisi ut aliquip ex ea commodo consequat. Duis aute irure dolor in reprehenderit in voluptate velit esse cillum dolore eu fugiat nulla pariatur. Excepteur sint occaecat cupidatat non proident, sunt in culpa qui officia deserunt mollit anim id est laborum.

Headline Headline Headline
Lorem ipsum dolor sit amet, consectetur adipisicing elit, sed do eiusmod tempor incididunt ut labore et dolore magna aliqua. Ut enim ad minim veniam, quis nostrud exercitation ullamco laboris nisi ut aliquip ex ea commodo consequat. Duis aute irure dolor in reprehenderit in voluptate velit esse cillum dolore eu fugiat nulla pariatur. Excepteur sint occaecat cupidatat non proident, sunt in culpa qui officia deserunt mollit anim id est laborum.
Lorem ipsum dolor sit amet, consectetur adipisicing elit, sed do eiusmod tempor incididunt ut labore et dolore magna aliqua. Ut enim ad minim veniam, quis nostrud exercitation ullamco laboris nisi ut aliquip ex ea commodo consequat. Duis aute irure dolor in reprehenderit in voluptate velit esse cillum dolore eu fugiat nulla pariatur. Excepteur sint occaecat cupidatat non proident, sunt in

Even spacing (left); Correct proximity (right).

Grids

A basic grid pattern imposes order on the layout. Grids align objects and space them properly which is pleasing to the eye. Used throughout, grids employ repetition to help the reader move through the book easily.

Grids help with consistency. For the most part, columns should be the same width and used to help the text fit within the grid. Images should be sized to fit the grid and maintain uniform distance from the text. Grids are determined by margins, columns, and the size of the page. The smaller the page, the fewer columns you can use comfortably before they become too narrow. The larger the page, the more columns you need to keep line lengths short enough to read easily.

In the example, you can see a 4x3 grid on the left-hand page, and a 3x3 grid on the right. Another possibility for smaller pages is a 4x4 grid.

Text can flow across two grid columns as seen on the left-hand page in the example labeled Filled-in grid, or, an image could fill two grid columns as seen on the right-hand page. A grid should not limit flexibility, rather, it should bring predictability to the page.

Lines, also called rules or strokes, should be of the same weight whenever they are used, with rare exceptions for emphasis (see Pull Quotes below).

In a page layout program, you can set up margins and columns in master pages—different master pages for different uses, such as the first page in a chapter, main body pages, and a final blank page, if needed.

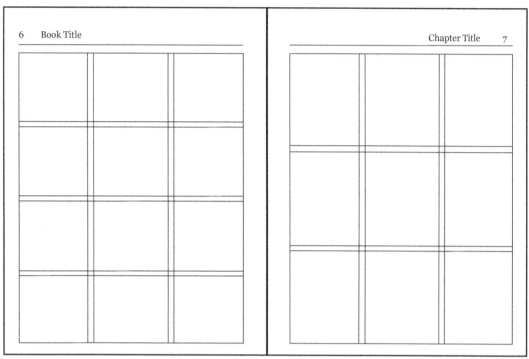

6   Book Title

Chapter Title   7

3x4 grid (left); 3x3 grid (right).

6   Book Title

Chapter Title   7

2x2 grid (left); 2x3 grid (right).

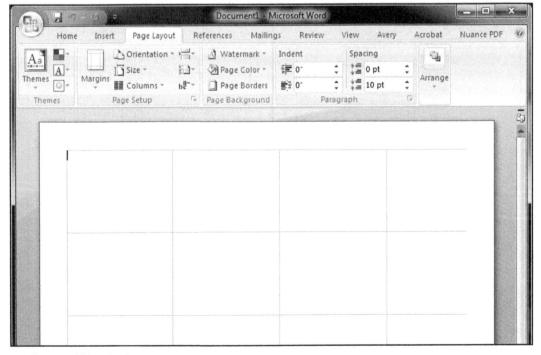

Filled-in grid.

4 Column grid in Word.

In a word processing program, you can establish the size of the grid squares and turn on the grid lines so that you can see them as you work. Word processing programs are not as flexible with layouts as page layout programs. You can design a good looking book using a word processing program, however, if you will learn the more advanced features of the software.

Margins

Set your margins to accommodate headers, footers, the text and images. In general, no element should violate the margins. All elements, headers, footers, page numbers, text and images must fit within the margins. Margins impose order and help create white space on the page.

When the Gutenburg bible was printed, margins were set so that facing pages were close together. That was the style of the times—to make a two-page spread look as if it were a single image.

With binding methods today, text set too close to the middle creates an optical illusion that the pages run together. Set a slightly larger margin toward the spine than on the outside. The smallest margin you should consider is a one half inch (.5") margin, and the larger the page size, the larger the margins should be.

Typical margin settings for a (in inches) 6 x 9 book are: top—1", inside—.75", outside—.625" and bottom—.625." On an 8.5 x 11 book, typical margins are:

Lorem ipsum dolor sit amet, consectetur adipisicing elit, sed do eiusmod tempor incididunt ut labore et dolore magna aliqua. Ut enim ad minim veniam, quis nostrud exercitation ullamco laboris nisi ut aliquip ex ea commodo consequat. Duis aute irure dolor in reprehenderit in voluptate velit esse cillum dolore eu fugiat nulla pariatur. Excepteur sint occaecat cupidatat non proident, sunt in culpa qui officia deserunt mollit anim id est laborum.

Lorem ipsum dolor sit amet, consectetur adipisicing elit, sed do eiusmod tempor incididunt ut labore et dolore magna aliqua. Ut enim ad minim veniam, quis nostrud exercitation ullamco laboris nisi ut aliquip ex ea commodo consequat. Duis aute irure dolor in reprehenderit in voluptate velit esse cillum dolore eu fugiat nulla pariatur. Excepteur sint occaecat cupidatat non proident, sunt in culpa qui officia deserunt mollit anim id est laborum.

Lorem ipsum dolor sit amet, consectetur adipisicing elit, sed do eiusmod tempor incididunt ut labore et dolore magna aliqua. Ut enim ad minim veniam, quis nostrud exercitation ullamco laboris nisi ut aliquip ex ea commodo consequat. Duis aute irure dolor in reprehenderit in voluptate velit esse cillum dolore eu fugiat nulla pariatur. Excepteur sint occaecat cupidatat non

aliquip ex ea commodo consequat. Duis aute irure dolor in reprehenderit in voluptate velit esse cillum dolore eu fugiat nulla pariatur. Excepteur sint occaecat cupidatat non proident, sunt in culpa qui officia deserunt mollit anim id est laborum.

Lorem ipsum dolor sit amet, consectetur adipisicing elit, sed do eiusmod tempor incididunt ut labore et dolore magna aliqua. Ut enim ad minim veniam, quis nostrud exercitation ullamco laboris nisi ut aliquip ex ea commodo consequat. Duis aute irure dolor in reprehenderit in voluptate velit esse cillum dolore eu fugiat nulla pariatur. Excepteur sint occaecat cupidatat non proident, sunt in culpa qui officia deserunt mollit anim id est laborum.

Lorem ipsum dolor sit amet, consectetur adipisicing elit, sed do eiusmod tempor incididunt ut labore et dolore magna aliqua. Ut enim ad minim veniam, quis nostrud exercitation ullamco laboris nisi ut aliquip ex ea commodo consequat. Duis aute irure dolor in reprehenderit in voluptate velit esse cillum dolore eu fugiat nulla pariatur. Excepteur sint occaecat cupidatat non proident, sunt in culpa qui officia deserunt mollit anim id est laborum.

Lorem ipsum dolor sit amet, consectetur adipisicing elit, sed do eiusmod tempor incididunt ut labore et

Margins in the Gutenburg bible.

Lorem ipsum dolor sit amet, consectetur adipisicing elit, sed do eiusmod tempor incididunt ut labore et dolore magna aliqua. Ut enim ad minim veniam, quis nostrud exercitation ullamco laboris nisi ut aliquip ex ea commodo consequat. Duis aute irure dolor in reprehenderit in voluptate velit esse cillum dolore eu fugiat nulla pariatur. Excepteur sint occaecat cupidatat non proident, sunt in culpa qui officia deserunt mollit anim id est laborum.

Lorem ipsum dolor sit amet, consectetur adipisicing elit, sed do eiusmod tempor incididunt ut labore et dolore magna aliqua. Ut enim ad minim veniam, quis nostrud exercitation ullamco laboris nisi ut aliquip ex ea commodo consequat. Duis aute irure dolor in reprehenderit in voluptate velit esse cillum dolore eu fugiat nulla pariatur. Excepteur sint occaecat cupidatat non proident, sunt in culpa qui officia deserunt mollit anim id est laborum.

Lorem ipsum dolor sit amet, consectetur adipisicing elit, sed do eiusmod tempor incididunt ut labore et dolore magna aliqua. Ut enim ad minim veniam, quis nostrud exercitation ullamco laboris nisi ut aliquip ex ea commodo consequat. Duis aute irure dolor in reprehenderit in voluptate velit esse cillum dolore eu fugiat nulla pariatur. Excepteur sint occaecat cupidatat non proident, sunt in culpa qui officia

Lorem ipsum dolor sit amet, consectetur adipisicing elit, sed do eiusmod tempor incididunt ut labore et dolore magna aliqua. Ut enim ad minim veniam, quis nostrud exercitation ullamco laboris nisi ut aliquip ex ea commodo consequat. Duis aute irure dolor in reprehenderit in voluptate velit esse cillum dolore eu fugiat nulla pariatur. Excepteur sint occaecat cupidatat non proident, sunt in culpa qui officia deserunt mollit anim id est laborum.

Lorem ipsum dolor sit amet, consectetur adipisicing elit, sed do eiusmod tempor incididunt ut labore et dolore magna aliqua. Ut enim ad minim veniam, quis nostrud exercitation ullamco laboris nisi ut aliquip ex ea commodo consequat. Duis aute irure dolor in reprehenderit in voluptate velit esse cillum dolore eu fugiat nulla pariatur. Excepteur sint occaecat cupidatat non proident, sunt in culpa qui officia deserunt mollit anim id est laborum.

Lorem ipsum dolor sit amet, consectetur adipisicing elit, sed do eiusmod tempor incididunt ut labore et dolore magna aliqua. Ut enim ad minim veniam, quis nostrud exercitation ullamco laboris nisi ut aliquip ex ea commodo consequat. Duis aute irure dolor in reprehenderit in voluptate velit esse cillum dolore eu fugiat nulla pariatur. Excepteur sint occaecat cupidatat non proident, sunt in culpa qui officia

Top margin allowing for the book title, chapter title and page number.

top—1.25" to 1.5", inside—1", outside—.75", and bottom—.75." The most common error is creating margins that are too narrow and of equal size.

Most books have running headers with the book's title on the left-hand page, and the chapter title on the right-hand page. Headers may also include the page numbers. If the header includes the page number, do not repeat page numbers in the footer.

In a page layout program, set up your master pages so that the top margin allows the book title or chapter title to rest above the text. In a word processor, choose one of the pre-installed headers for left and right pages and enter the appropriate text.

Page Numbers

Place page numbers in either the header or footer. Typically they are placed at the outside edge or in the center of the page, but not at the spine edge. It is difficult to locate page numbers while flipping through the book if they are near the spine.

Page numbers in the front matter (title page, table of contents, and so on) are given in lowercase Roman numerals, so the first half-title page would be page i. Page numbers beginning with the introduction are given in Arabic numerals, so the first page of the introduction would be page 1, although some publishers continue page numbering from the front matter.

Columns

Columns are the easiest way to control line length. Text stretching too far across the page is difficult for the reader to follow. Pages six inches wide or narrower can be set in a single column, but larger books need two or more columns.

Columns have two components—distance between (gutter) and width (line length). Try to keep line lengths from 60 to 70 characters. Columns do not have to be equal in width, but most often they look best when they are. In both page layout programs and word processors, you can adjust the number of columns, the line length, and the distance between the columns. A distance of one quarter of an inch (.25") is a good starting place. Too much distance between columns looks awkward, and too little distance between columns makes the text difficult to read, as you can see in the example on the previous page.

Images

Adding images to a page can present layout challenges, especially if the image does not fit neatly into the grid. Your book will look best if they do, however, so you may need to re-scan at a larger size or crop images down to fit.

Avoid placing images so that their edges end in the middle of grid squares causing narrow columns of text to form beside the image. Neither should images and text fill grid columns incompletely leaving awkward white space as seen on the right-hand page in the example (next page).

---

6   Book Title

Lorem ipsum dolor sit amet, consectetur adipisicing elit, sed do eiusmod tempor incididunt ut labore et dolore magna aliqua. Ut enim ad minim veniam, quis nostrud exercitation ullamco laboris nisi ut aliquip ex ea commodo consequat. Duis aute irure dolor in reprehenderit in voluptate velit esse cillum dolore eu fugiat nulla pariatur. Excepteur sint occaecat cupidatat non proident, sunt in culpa qui officia deserunt mollit anim id est laborum.

Lorem ipsum dolor sit amet, consectetur adipisicing elit, sed do eiusmod tempor incididunt ut labore et dolore magna aliqua. Ut enim ad minim veniam, quis nostrud exercitation ullamco laboris nisi ut aliquip ex ea commodo consequat. Duis aute irure dolor in reprehenderit in voluptate velit esse cillum dolore eu fugiat nulla pariatur. Excepteur sint occaecat cupidatat non proident, sunt in culpa qui officia

deserunt mollit anim id est laborum.

Lorem ipsum dolor sit amet, consectetur adipisicing elit, sed do eiusmod tempor incididunt ut labore et dolore magna aliqua. Ut enim ad minim veniam, quis nostrud exercitation ullamco laboris nisi ut aliquip ex ea commodo consequat. Duis aute irure dolor in reprehenderit in voluptate velit esse cillum dolore eu fugiat nulla pariatur. Excepteur sint occaecat cupidatat non proident, sunt in culpa qui officia deserunt mollit anim id est laborum.

Lorem ipsum dolor sit amet, consectetur adipisicing elit, sed do eiusmod tempor incididunt ut labore et dolore magna aliqua. Ut enim ad minim veniam, quis nostrud exercitation ullamco laboris nisi ut aliquip ex ea commodo consequat. Duis aute irure dolor in reprehenderit in voluptate velit

---

Chapter Title   7

Lorem ipsum dolor sit amet, consectetur adipisicing elit, sed do eiusmod tempor incididunt ut labore et dolore magna aliqua. Ut enim ad minim veniam, quis nostrud exercitation ullamco laboris nisi ut aliquip ex ea commodo consequat. Duis aute irure dolor in reprehenderit in voluptate velit esse cillum dolore eu fugiat nulla pariatur. Excepteur sint occaecat cupidatat non proident, sunt in culpa qui officia deserunt mollit anim id est laborum.

Lorem ipsum dolor sit amet, consectetur adipisicing elit, sed do eiusmod tempor incididunt ut labore et dolore magna aliqua. Ut enim ad minim veniam, quis nostrud exercitation ullamco laboris nisi ut aliquip ex ea commodo consequat. Duis aute irure dolor in reprehenderit in voluptate velit esse cillum dolore eu fugiat nulla pariatur. Excepteur sint occaecat cupidatat non proident, sunt in culpa qui officia deserunt mollit anim id est laborum.

Lorem ipsum dolor sit amet, consectetur adipisicing elit, sed do eiusmod tempor incididunt ut labore et dolore magna aliqua. Ut enim ad minim veniam, quis nostrud exercitation ullamco laboris nisi ut aliquip ex ea commodo consequat. Duis aute irure dolor in reprehenderit in voluptate velit esse cillum dolore eu fugiat nulla pariatur. Excepteur sint occaecat cupidatat non proident, sunt in culpa qui officia deserunt mollit anim id est laborum.

Lorem ipsum dolor sit amet, consectetur adipisicing elit, sed do eiusmod tempor incididunt ut labore et dolore magna aliqua. Ut enim ad minim veniam, quis nostrud exercitation ullamco laboris nisi ut aliquip ex ea commodo consequat. Duis aute irure dolor in reprehenderit in voluptate velit esse cillum dolore eu fugiat nulla pariatur. Excepteur sint occaecat cupidatat non proident, sunt in culpa qui officia deserunt mollit anim id est laborum.

Columns incorrectly spaced; too far (left); too close (right).

SET YOURSELF UP TO SELF-PUBLISH

Lorem ipsum dolor sit amet, consectetur adipisicing elit, sed do eiusmod tempor incididunt ut labore et dolore magna aliqua. Ut enim ad minim veniam, quis nostrud exercitation ullamco laboris nisi ut aliquip ex ea commodo consequat. Duis aute irure dolor in reprehenderit in voluptate velit esse cillum dolore eu fugiat nulla pariatur. Excepteur sint occaecat cupidatat non proident, sunt in culpa qui officia deserunt mollit anim id est laborum.

Lorem ipsum dolor sit amet, consectetur adipisicing elit, sed do eiusmod tempor incididunt ut labore et dolore magna aliqua. Ut enim ad minim veniam, quis nostrud exercitation ullamco laboris nisi ut aliquip ex ea commodo consequat. Duis aute irure dolor in reprehenderit in voluptate velit esse cillum dolore eu fugiat nulla pariatur. Excepteur sint occaecat cupidatat non proident, sunt in culpa qui officia deserunt mollit anim id est laborum.

Lorem ipsum dolor sit amet, consectetur adipisicing elit, sed do eiusmod tempor incididunt ut labore et dolore magna aliqua. Ut enim ad minim veniam,

Lorem ipsum dolor sit amet, consectetur adipisicing elit, sed do eiusmod tempor incididunt ut labore et dolore magna aliqua. Ut enim ad minim veniam, quis nostrud exercitation ullamco laboris nisi ut aliquip ex ea commodo consequat. Duis aute irure dolor in reprehenderit in voluptate velit esse cillum dolore eu fugiat nulla pariatur. Excepteur sint occaecat cupidatat non proident, sunt in culpa qui officia deserunt mollit anim id est laborum.

Lorem ipsum dolor sit amet, consectetur adipisicing elit, sed do eiusmod tempor incididunt ut labore et dolore magna aliqua. Ut enim ad minim veniam, quis nostrud exercitation ullamco laboris nisi ut aliquip ex ea commodo consequat. Duis aute irure dolor in reprehenderit in voluptate velit esse cillum dolore eu fugiat nulla pariatur. Excepteur sint occaecat

cupidatat non proident, sunt in culpa qui officia deserunt mollit anim id est laborum.

Lorem ipsum dolor sit amet, consectetur adipisicing elit, sed do eiusmod tempor incididunt ut labore et dolore magna aliqua. Ut enim ad minim veniam, quis nostrud exercitation ullamco laboris nisi ut aliquip ex ea commodo consequat. Duis aute veniam, quis nostrud exercitation ullamco laboris nisi ut aliquip ex commodo consequat. Duis aute irure dolor in reprehenderit in voluptate velit esse cillum dolore eu fugiat nulla pariatur. Excepteur sint occaecat cupidatat non proident, sunt in culpa qui

officia deserunt mollit anim id est laborum.

Lorem ipsum dolor sit amet, consectetur adipisicing elit, sed do eiusmod tempor incididunt ut labore et dolore magna aliqua. Ut enim ad minim veniam, quis nostrud exercitation ullamco laboris nisi ut

Lorem ipsum dolor sit amet, consectetur adipisicing elit, sed do eiusmod tempor incididunt ut labore et dolore magna aliqua. Ut

Grid filled incorrectly.

Lorem ipsum dolor sit amet, consectetur adipisicing elit, sed do eiusmod tempor incididunt ut labore et dolore magna aliqua. Ut enim ad minim veniam, quis nostrud exercitation ullamco laboris nisi ut aliquip ex ea commodo consequat. Duis aute irure dolor in reprehenderit in voluptate velit esse cillum dolore eu fugiat nulla pariatur. Excepteur sint occaecat cupidatat non proident, sunt in culpa qui officia deserunt mollit anim id est laborum.

Lorem ipsum dolor sit amet, consectetur adipisicing elit, sed do eiusmod tempor incididunt ut labore et dolore magna aliqua. Ut enim ad minim veniam, quis nostrud exercitation ullamco laboris nisi ut aliquip ex ea commodo consequat. Duis aute irure dolor in reprehenderit in voluptate velit esse cillum dolore eu fugiat nulla pariatur. Excepteur sint occaecat cupidatat non proident, sunt in culpa qui officia deserunt mollit anim id est laborum.

Lorem ipsum dolor sit amet, consectetur adipisicing elit, sed do eiusmod tempor incididunt ut labore et dolore magna aliqua. Ut enim ad minim veniam, quis nostrud exercitation ullamco laboris nisi ut aliquip ex ea commodo consequat. Duis aute irure dolor in reprehenderit in voluptate velit esse cillum dolore eu fugiat nulla pariatur. Excepteur sint occaecat cupidatat non proident, sunt in culpa qui officia

Lorem ipsum dolor sit amet, consectetur adipisicing elit, sed do eiusmod tempor incididunt ut labore et dolore magna aliqua. Ut enim ad minim veniam, quis nostrud exercitation ullamco laboris nisi ut aliquip ex ea commodo consequat. Duis aute irure dolor in reprehenderit in voluptate velit esse cillum

Lorem ipsum dolor sit amet, consectetur adipisicing elit, sed do eiusmod tempor incididunt ut labore et dolore magna aliqua. Ut enim ad minim veniam, quis nostrud

Lorem ipsum dolor sit amet, consectetur adipisicing elit, sed do eiusmod tempor incididunt ut labore et dolore magna aliqua. Ut enim ad minim veniam, quis nostrud exercitation ullamco laboris nisi ut aliquip ex ea commodo consequat. Duis aute irure dolor in reprehenderit in voluptate velit esse cillum dolore eu fugiat nulla pariatur. Excepteur sint occaecat cupidatat non proident, sunt in culpa qui officia deserunt mollit anim id est laborum.

Lorem ipsum dolor sit amet, consectetur adipisicing elit, sed do eiusmod tempor incididunt ut labore et dolore magna aliqua. Ut enim ad min im veniam, quis nostrud

cupidatat non proident, sunt in culpa qui officia deserunt mollit anim id est laborum.

Lorem ipsum dolor sit amet, consectetur adipisicing elit, sed do eiusmod tempor incididunt ut labore et dolore magna aliqua. Ut enim ad minim veniam, quis nostrud

exercitation ullamco laboris nisi ut aliquip ex ea commodo consequat. Duis aute irure dolor in reprehenderit in voluptate velit esse cillum dolore eu fugiat nulla pariatur. Excepteur sint occaecat cupidatat non proident, sunt in culpa qui officia deserunt mol-

Grid filled correctly.

Most images can stand a bit of cropping. In fact, many images are stronger after they are cropped because the subject of the image takes center stage.

Size indicates relative importance. Try to keep this in mind when choosing images. The bigger the image, the more important the reader will think it is to the story.

Images need space around them. In most cases, the space between the columns serves as a good rule for the space to leave around your images. If the space between your columns is one quarter of one inch (.25"), use the text wrap feature to give the image space on every side except the side where you want to place a caption. Captions, because they belong to the photo, should be closer (see below).

Note: Captions and credits are not the same. Captions explain who or what is in the image. Credits acknowledge who owns or has possession of the image. Captions should be with the image on the page, aligned left beginning at the left edge of the photograph, not centered underneath. Centering captions creates visual obstacles for the reader. Credits can be given on the page with the image just after the caption, or in a list of credits at the end of the book or each chapter.

If you want to add fancy photo corners or edge effects to your images, do so in your image editing software after you have re-sized the image for its spot within the grid. Pick one or two fancy effects, and stick with them for consistency.

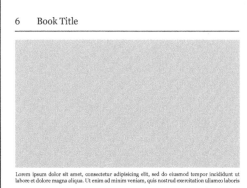
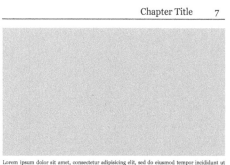

Images with captions.

Advanced Page Layouts

What follows are advanced layout options often found in non-fiction books. Use them for visual interest, but only if they benefit the reader in some way.

Pull Quotes

Pull quotes are used by magazines to entice readers to stop flipping pages and start reading. They are an opportunity for a little creativity on the page. In a book they can be used effectively, although they should be used sparingly.

Side Bars

Sidebars are another way to use your grid to add information that you may not want to include within the narrative. It may be information about a photograph that is too long for a simple caption, or something you want the reader to know alongside the narrative (see the example opposite).

If you take the time to create a basic page layout that is easy to flow text and place images into, your book will look better than most. Look through your personal library and find a simple layout that you like. Look at books of the same physical size—it can be hard to match layouts if you do not.

Now that you have a feel for the general layout of the page, the next chapter will explore the fundamentals of typesetting.

6   Book Title

Lorem ipsum dolor sit amet, consectetur adipisicing elit, sed do eiusmod tempor incididunt ut labore et dolore magna aliqua. Ut enim ad minim veniam, quis nostrud exercitation ullamco laboris nisi ut aliquip ex ea commodo consequat. Duis aute irure dolor in reprehenderit in voluptate velit esse cillum dolore eu fugiat nulla pariatur. Excepteur sint occaecat cupidatat non proident, sunt in culpa qui officia deserunt mollit anim id est laborum.

Lorem ipsum dolor sit amet, consectetur adipisicing elit, sed do eiusmod tempor incididunt ut labore et dolore magna aliqua. Ut enim ad minim veniam, quis nostrud exercitation ullamco laboris nisi ut aliquip ex ea commodo consequat. Duis aute irure dolor in reprehenderit in voluptate velit esse cillum dolore re eu fugiat nulla pariatur. Excepteur sint occaecat cupidatat non proident, sunt in culpa qui officia deserunt mollit anim id est laborum.

Lorem ipsum dolor sit amet, consectetur adipisicing elit, sed do eiusmod tempor incididunt ut labore et dolore magna aliqua. Ut enim ad minim veniam, quis nostrud exercitation ullamco laboris nisi ut aliquip ex ea commodo consequat. Duis aute irure dolor in reprehenderit in voluptate velit esse cil-

Lorem ipsum dolor sit amet

lum dolore eu fugiat nulla pariatur. Excepteur sint occaecat cupidatat non proident, sunt in culpa qui officia deserunt mollit anim id est laborum.

Lorem ipsum dolor sit amet, consectetur adipisicing elit, sed do eiusmod tempor incididunt ut labore et dolore magna aliqua. Ut enim ad minim veniam, quis nostrud exercitation ullamco laboris nisi ut aliquip ex ea commodo consequat. Duis aute irure dolor in reprehenderit in voluptate velit esse cillum dolore eu fugiat nulla pariatur. Excepteur sint occaecat cupidatat non proident, sunt in culpa qui officia deserunt mollit anim id est laborum.

Lorem ipsum dolor sit amet, consectetur adipisicing elit, sed do eiusmod tempor incididunt ut labore et dolore magna aliqua. Ut enim ad minim veniam, quis nostrud exercitation ullamco laboris nisi ut aliquip ex ea commodo consequat. Duis aute irure dolor in reprehenderit in voluptate velit esse cillum dolore eu fugiat nulla pariatur. Excepteur sint occaecat cupidatat non proident, sunt in culpa qui officia deserunt mollit anim id est laborum.Ut

Chapter Title   7

Lorem ipsum dolor sit amet, consectetur adipisicing elit, sed do eiusmod tempor incididunt ut labore et dolore magna aliqua. Ut enim ad minim veniam, quis nostrud exercitation ullamco laboris nisi ut aliquip ex ea commodo consequat. Duis aute irure dolor in reprehenderit in voluptate velit esse cillum dolore eu fugiat nulla pariatur. Excepteur sint occaecat cupidatat non proident, sunt in culpa qui officia deserunt mollit anim id est laborum.

Lorem ipsum dolor sit amet, consectetur adipisicing elit, sed do eiusmod tempor incididunt ut labore et dolore magna aliqua. Ut enim ad minim veniam, quis nostrud exercitation ullamco laboris nisi ut aliquip ex ea commodo consequat. Duis aute irure dolor in reprehenderit in voluptate velit esse cillum dolore eu fugiat nulla pariatur. Excep-

Lorem ipsum dolor sit amet

teur sint occaecat cupidatat non proident, sunt in culpa qui officia deserunt mollit anim id est laborum.

Lorem ipsum dolor sit amet, consectetur adipisicing elit, sed do eiusmod tempor incididunt ut labore et dolore magna aliqua. Ut enim ad minim ve-

niam, quis nostrud exercitation ullamco laboris nisi ut aliquip ex ea commodo consequat. Duis aute irure dolor in reprehenderit in voluptate velit esse cillum dolore eu fugiat nulla pariatur. Excepteur sint occaecat cupidatat non proident, sunt in culpa qui officia deserunt mollit anim id est laborum.

Lorem ipsum dolor sit amet, consectetur adipisicing elit, sed do eiusmod tempor incididunt ut labore et dolore magna aliqua. Ut enim ad minim veniam, quis nostrud exercitation ullamco laboris nisi ut aliquip ex ea commodo consequat. Duis aute irure dolor in reprehenderit in voluptate velit esse cillum dolore eu fugiat nulla pariatur. Excepteur sint occaecat cupidatat non proident, sunt in culpa qui officia deserunt mollit anim id est laborum.

Lorem ipsum dolor sit amet, consectetur adipisicing elit, sed do eiusmod tempor incididunt ut labore et dolore magna aliqua. Ut enim ad minim veniam, quis nostrud exercitation ullamco laboris nisi ut aliquip ex ea commodo consequat. Duis aute irure dolor in reprehenderit in voluptate velit esse cillum dolore eu fugiat nulla pariatur. Excepteur sint occaecat cupidatat non proident, sunt in culpa qui officia deserunt mollit anim id est laborum.

Lorem ipsum dolor sit amet, consectetur adipisicing elit, sed do eiusmod tempor incididunt ut labore et dolore magna aliqua. Ut enim ad minim ve-

Pull-quotes across columns (left); Pull-quotes within a column (right).

6   Book Title

Lorem ipsum dolor sit amet, consectetur adipisicing elit, sed do eiusmod tempor incididunt ut labore et dolore magna aliqua. Ut enim ad minim veniam, quis nostrud exercitation ullamco laboris nisi ut aliquip ex ea commodo consequat. Duis aute irure dolor in reprehenderit in voluptate velit esse cillum dolore eu fugiat nulla pariatur. Excepteur sint occaecat cupidatat non proident, sunt in culpa qui officia deserunt mollit anim id est laborum.

Lorem ipsum dolor sit amet, consectetur adipisicing elit, sed do eiusmod tempor incididunt ut labore et dolore magna aliqua. Ut enim ad minim veniam, quis nostrud exercitation ullamco laboris nisi ut aliquip ex ea commodo consequat. Duis aute irure dolor in reprehenderit in voluptate velit esse cillum dolore eu fugiat nulla pariatur. Excepteur sint occaecat cupidatat non proident, sunt in culpa qui officia deserunt mollit anim id est laborum.

Lorem ipsum dolor sit amet, consectetur adipisicing elit, sed do eiusmod tempor incididunt ut labore et dolore magna aliqua. Ut enim ad minim veniam, quis nostrud exercitation ullamco laboris nisi ut aliquip ex ea commodo consequat. Duis aute irure dolor in reprehenderit in voluptate velit esse cillum dolore eu fugiat nulla pariatur. Excepteur sint occaecat cupidatat non proident, sunt in culpa qui officia deserunt mollit anim id est laborum.

Lorem ipsum dolor sit amet, consectetur adipisicing elit, sed do eiusmod tempor incididunt ut labore et dolore magna aliqua. Ut enim ad minim veniam, quis nostrud exercitation ullamco laboris nisi ut aliquip ex ea commodo consequat. Duis aute irure dolor in reprehenderit in voluptate velit esse cillum dolore eu fugiat nulla pariatur. Excepteur sint occaecat cupidatat non proident, sunt in culpa qui officia deserunt mollit anim id est laborum.

- Lorem ipsum dolor sit amet
- Consectetur adipisicing elit
- Sed do eiusmod tempor
- Incididunt ut labore
- Magna aliqua
- Ut enim ad minim veniam
- Quis nostrud exercitation

Chapter Title   7

Lorem ipsum dolor cupidatat non proident, sit amet, consectetur sunt in culpa qui officia adipisicing elit, sed do deserunt mollit anim id eiusmod tempor incidi- est laborum. dunt ut labore et dolore magna aliqua. Ut enim ad minim veniam, quis nostrud exercitation ullamco laboris nisi ut aliquip ex ea commodo consequat. Duis aute irure dolor in repre- henderit in voluptate velit esse cillum dolore eu fugiat nulla pariatur. Excepteur sint occaecat cupidatat non proident, sunt in culpa qui officia deserunt mollit anim id est laborum.

Lorem ipsum dolor sit amet, consectetur adipisicing elit, sed do eiusmod tempor incidi- dunt ut labore et dolore magna aliqua. Ut enim adipisicing elit, sed do nostrud exercitation ullamco laboris nisi ut aliquip ex ea commodo consequat. Duis aute irure dolor in repre- henderit in voluptate velit esse cillum dolore eu fugiat nulla pariatur. Excepteur sint occaecat

Lorem ipsum dolor sit amet, consectetur adipisicing elit, sed do eiusmod tempor incidi- dunt ut labore et dolore magna aliqua. Ut enim ad minim veniam, quis nostrud exercitation ullamco laboris nisi ut aliquip ex ea commodo consequat. Duis aute irure dolor in repre- henderit in voluptate velit esse cillum dolore eu fugiat nulla pariatur. Excepteur sint occaecat cupidatat non proident, sunt in culpa qui officia deserunt mollit anim id est laborum.Ut

Lorem ipsum dolor sit amet, consectetur adipisicing elit, sed do eiusmod tempor incidi- dunt ut labore et dolore magna aliqua. Ut enim ad minim veniam, quis nostrud exercitation ullamco laboris nisi ut aliquip ex ea commodo

Text spread across two columns with a side bar (left); Three columns (right).

Chapter 7

Typesetting for Print

Typesetting conventions have developed over the last 400 years to make books both beautiful and easy to read. If you mess with the rules of readability, reading comprehension drops dramatically.

The rest of this chapter will help you avoid leaving little clues that the book is "self-published."

The Basics

Before you can start typesetting the different parts of your book, you need a good understanding of what affects reading comprehension.

The Rules of Readability

In addition to hundreds of years of publishing tradition, modern studies have determined what affects our ability to read and comprehend type. The rules that follow are based upon the results of tradition, observation and studies.

Use serif fonts, also called typefaces. Twice as many readers are able to easily understand words printed in serif typefaces. Serif fonts have small extenders between letters. Sans serif typefaces are easier to read on the screen, so these fonts are fine for websites and electronic communications, but stick to serif fonts for printed books.

High contrast is best. Black type on a white page is optimal. Even dark blues and browns are more difficult to read than black. Avoid placing type on a colored background unless it the background is very light. And, avoid reverse outs. It is difficult for readers to digest white type on a black background for more than a one- or two-word headline.

Avoid all capitals (all caps). Not only do readers feel as if you are shouting at them, we recognize words based upon the top half of the letters. Letters in all caps lack the characteristic upper extenders and rounded forms we use to recognize whole words at a time, so text in all caps slows reading to a crawl.

Give the letters room to breathe. Squeezing type together makes text uncomfortable, if not impossible, to read.

Use bold sparingly. Headlines and subheads in bold help the reader skim through the material, but large blocks of type in bold looks dense and is difficult to read.

> "A brilliant piece of graphic design which goes unread is a waste of paper, ink, money and effort, and perhaps above all, a lost opportunity to communicate something of value."
>
> **Colin Wheildon and Mal Warwick**
> *Type & Layout: How Typography and Design Can Get Your Message*
> *Across or Get In the Way*

Fonts

Typography does not have to be sophisticated to look good and read easily. Typefaces often come in families that include Roman (plain), italics, bold and bold italics. A few font families will also have black (heavy) or light (narrow).

Choose a serif typeface for the main body of the book. These are common serif typefaces used in books: Adobe Caslon, Adobe Garamond, Baskerville Old Face, Bookman Old Style, Goudy Old Style, Palatino, and Utopia.

Common Body Text Fonts	Common Headline Fonts
Adobe Caslon	Franklin Gothic Book
Adobe Garamond	Gill Sans
Baskerville Old Face	Hypatia Sans Pro
Bookman Old Style	Myriad Pro
Goudy Oldstyle	Tahoma
Palatino	

Gill Sans	Franklin Gothic Book
Adobe Caslon	Goudy Old Style
Myriad Pro	**Tahoma**
Baskerville	Palatino
Hypatia Sans	
Bookman	

Common body and headline fonts (left); Font pairs (right).

You can keep the same font for headlines and subheads, but make them bolder and bigger, or you can use a sans serif typeface. If you prefer a sans serif font, choose one that creates a good contrast with your body text font. Weak contrasts do not look as good as strong contrasts.

These are common sans serif headline fonts: Franklin Gothic Book, Gill Sans, Hypathia Sans Pro, Myriad Pro, Nimbus Sans, Segoe and Tahoma.

Fonts to avoid: Times New Roman and Helvetica (both are newspaper fonts meant for narrow columns), Arial (overused), Copperplate (all caps), Courier (unless you want to look like you have used a typewriter), Papyrus (so overused it has become a cliché), Brush Script, Comic Sans, Curlz, anything that implies handwriting, and fonts supposed to make one think of the Dark Ages, the Middle Ages, the Renaissance, or the Book of Kells.

Avoid script fonts, even for something personal such as a transcription of a letter or a page from a diary. Loosely set script fonts may be fine for chapter titles but are difficult to read for more than a few words. Italics in one of the basic book fonts will distinguish itself enough to make a transcription stand out.

There are three major font file types: Open Type, TrueType and Postscript. Apple opened the world of scalable type design with its TrueType fonts. Adobe got into the game a bit later with its Type1 (Postscript) fonts. OpenType has been a collaboration of Microsoft and Adobe and looks to be winning over publishers and printers.

Some fonts require purchase in order to use them; others come pre-installed in your word processing or page layout programs already licensed for you to use. Avoid free fonts available on the Internet (mostly TrueType). Some have serious technical issues that you will not want to discover after your book is printed.

Avoid any font that will not embed into a PDF (portable document format—the file type most commonly requested by printers). If you do not have a license for your fonts, they will not save correctly into a PDF. If you are unsure, type a few words in each of your chosen fonts and convert that test file into a PDF. Most word processors will save files to PDFs using a simple "save as" command. If no error messages appear, the fonts are most probably all right.

There is no need to go wild with fonts. It is rare to use more than two to three fonts in a book's interior. Stick to the commonly-used book fonts. You can be a little more creative with the font on the cover.

Type Size

For the main body of the book, make the font size big enough to read easily, and appropriate to the column width. Narrower columns can handle smaller fonts.

For adults, most fonts are readable between point sizes 10 and 12. Smaller font sizes are difficult to read. Smaller type is fine for captions or footnotes, down to 7 or 8 points, depending upon the font. Larger font sizes, 14 points or larger, should be reserved for large print books made for people with impaired vision. Larger font sizes are acceptable for headlines and subheads.

Leading

The term leading comes from a time when type was set by hand and thin strips of lead divided lines horizontally to create a space above and below each line.

Standard leading is two points greater than the type height for standard text and proportionally larger with larger sized text. Your body text may be 12 points tall with 14 point leading, whereas your cover font could be 48 points tall with 58 point leading—an amount proportional to the size of the large letters.

One way to decrease the density on the page (or lengthen a manuscript) is to increase the leading. Increasing the leading too much, however, will look like double spacing which is not attractive.

Emphasis

It is always better to make the reader feel emphasis with your words rather than using typesetting tricks. Italics is the most common way to show emphasis. Italics is also used to highlight foreign words, indicate book or movie titles, and the thoughts of a character—a rare occurrence in non-fiction.

Use bold, if you must, but only for short phrases. Paragraph after paragraph of bold text looks dense and uninviting.

Keep the exclamation points under control. If everything is important, nothing is—relatively. Avoid all capitals in running text unless you want the reader to feel that you are shouting your message.

There is no need to put everyday expressions in quotes, except to indicate irony. When air quotes became a popular hand gesture, they also proliferated in printed works. Try not to litter your book with unnecessary quotes. Save them for the places where you are actually quoting another author.

Avoid underlining, except as hyperlinks. Underlining had a place when typewriters offered little else, but underlining is not used for emphasis today.

Case

In English, when to use upper case and when to use lower case is fairly straight forward. Sentence case is used in paragraphs where capital letters begin sentences. Title case is used for headlines and subheads only. In title case, most words are capitalized except prepositions (by, to, from, of, on, with, at), articles (a, an, the), and coordinating conjunctions (and, but, or, for, and nor).

Capitals are used for proper nouns, such as the names of people (George Washington), businesses (General Motors), specific places (Savannah, America, the Mississippi Delta), nationalities (German), languages (French) and religions (Methodist).

Job or honorary titles are capitalized, but only when it refers to a specific person and precedes their name. So, there are presidents elected in the United States, but President Lincoln gets a capital in his title.

Capitals, like commas, can run amok. In book publishing, fewer capitals are preferred. If in doubt, use the lowercase letter.

Letter Spacing and Kerning

Letter spacing and kerning affect the distance between letters. Letter spacing (tracking) affects the spacing between all letters. Adjusting the letter spacing can open up the look of a page and make some fonts easier to read. In most cases, however, your software will correctly determine letter spacing. On occasion, altering letter spacing can help avoid orphans (more on this shortly).

Kerning adjusts the spacing between two, side-by-side letters to make them look more natural sitting next to each other. The auto-kerning feature in most software is fine for most body text. Kerning individual pairs of letters may be important, however, to make the large letters on your cover look their best.

open letter spacing
normal letter spacing
closed letter spacing

WA **W A**
kerned   not kerned

Letter spacing (left); Kerning (right).

Titles, Headlines and Subheads

Titles, headlines and subheads are about hierarchy—clues to what is the most important. At the top of the hierarchy (and also in the largest font size and strength) are the chapter titles. Next are the headlines that should be bigger and bolder than subheads. If needed, create sub-subheads down to a second or third level.

The lowest level could be a run-in subhead where the subhead does not sit above the paragraph, but begins the paragraph and ends in a period (see below).

For most books, headlines and subheads should be aligned flush left. Centered or right-aligned headlines and subheads can work (albeit a challenge), but only over fully justified paragraphs. Whichever style you choose, be consistent.

Keep headlines and subheads short and sweet. Avoid having them run onto a second line, if possible. Headlines and subheads do not end in punctuation, except if you are using a run-in subhead, such as:

Tuesday. On the first sunny morning in a month, ...
Wednesday. We began to harvest ...

Aesthetically, headlines and subheads are never stacked one on top of another. There is always a paragraph in between them.

Set Yourself Up to Self-Publish

Lorem ipsum dolor sit amet, consectetur adipisicing elit, sed do eiusmod tempor incididunt ut labore et dolore magna aliqua. Ut enim ad minim veniam, quis nostrud exercitation ullamco laboris nisi ut aliquip ex ea commodo consequat. Duis aute irure dolor in reprehenderit in voluptate velit esse cillum dolore eu fugiat nulla pariatur. Excepteur sint occaecat cupidatat non proident, sunt in culpa qui officia deserunt mollit anim id est laborum.

Headline Headline Headline

Lorem ipsum dolor sit amet, consectetur adipisicing elit, sed do eiusmod tempor incididunt ut labore et dolore magna aliqua. Ut enim ad minim veniam, quis nostrud exercitation ullamco laboris nisi ut aliquip ex ea commodo consequat. Duis aute irure dolor in reprehenderit in voluptate velit esse cillum dolore eu fugiat nulla pariatur. Excepteur sint occaecat cupidatat non proident, sunt in culpa qui officia deserunt mollit anim id est laborum.

Subhead Subhead Subhead Subhead

Lorem ipsum dolor sit amet, consectetur adipisicing elit, sed do eiusmod tempor incididunt ut labore et dolore magna aliqua. Ut enim ad minim veniam, quis nostrud exercitation ullamco laboris nisi ut aliquip ex ea commodo consequat. Duis aute irure dolor in reprehenderit in voluptate velit esse cillum dolore eu fugiat nulla pariatur. Excepteur sint occaecat cupidatat non proident, sunt in culpa qui officia deserunt mollit anim id est laborum.

Sub-Subhead Sub-Subhead Sub-Subhead Subhead

Lorem ipsum dolor sit amet, consectetur adipisicing elit, sed do eiusmod tempor incididunt ut labore et dolore magna aliqua. Ut enim ad minim veniam, quis nostrud exercitation ullamco laboris nisi ut aliquip ex ea commodo consequat. Duis aute irure dolor in

Lorem ipsum dolor sit amet, consectetur adipisicing elit, sed do eiusmod tempor incididunt ut labore et dolore magna aliqua. Ut enim ad minim veniam, quis nostrud exercitation ullamco laboris nisi ut aliquip ex ea commodo consequat. Duis aute irure dolor in reprehenderit in voluptate velit esse cillum dolore eu fugiat nulla pariatur. Excepteur sint occaecat cupidatat non proident, sunt in culpa qui officia deserunt mollit anim id est laborum.

Headline Headline Headline

Lorem ipsum dolor sit amet, consectetur adipisicing elit, sed do eiusmod tempor incididunt ut labore et dolore magna aliqua. Ut enim ad minim veniam, quis nostrud exercitation ullamco laboris nisi ut aliquip ex ea commodo consequat. Duis aute irure dolor in reprehenderit in voluptate velit esse cillum dolore eu fugiat nulla pariatur. Excepteur sint occaecat cupidatat non proident, sunt in culpa qui officia deserunt mollit anim id est laborum.

Subhead Subhead Subhead Subhead

Lorem ipsum dolor sit amet, consectetur adipisicing elit, sed do eiusmod tempor incididunt ut labore et dolore magna aliqua. Ut enim ad minim veniam, quis nostrud exercitation ullamco laboris nisi ut aliquip ex ea commodo consequat. Duis aute irure dolor in reprehenderit in voluptate velit esse cillum dolore eu fugiat nulla pariatur. Excepteur sint occaecat cupidatat non proident, sunt in culpa qui officia deserunt mollit anim id est laborum.

Sub-Subhead Sub-Subhead Sub-Subhead Subhead

Lorem ipsum dolor sit amet, consectetur adipisicing elit, sed do eiusmod tempor incididunt ut labore et dolore magna aliqua. Ut enim ad minim veniam, quis nostrud exercitation ullamco laboris nisi ut aliquip ex ea commodo consequat. Duis aute irure dolor in

Headlines and subheads.

Lorem ipsum dolor sit amet, consectetur adipisicing elit, sed do eiusmod tempor incididunt ut labore et dolore magna aliqua. Ut enim ad minim veniam, quis nostrud exercitation ullamco laboris nisi ut aliquip ex ea commodo consequat. Duis aute irure dolor in reprehenderit in voluptate velit esse cillum dolore eu fugiat nulla pariatur. Excepteur sint occaecat cupidatat non proident, sunt in culpa qui officia deserunt mollit anim id est laborum.

Lorem ipsum dolor sit amet, consectetur adipisicing elit, sed do eiusmod tempor incididunt ut labore et dolore magna aliqua. Ut enim ad minim veniam, quis nostrud exercitation ullamco laboris nisi ut aliquip ex ea commodo consequat. Duis aute irure dolor in voluptate velit esse cillum dolore eu fugiat nulla pariatur. Ex-

cepteur sint occaecat cupidatat non proident, sunt in culpa qui officia deserunt mollit anim id est laborum.

Lorem ipsum dolor sit amet, consectetur adipisicing elit, sed do eiusmod tempor incididunt ut labore et dolore magna aliqua. Ut enim ad minim veniam, quis nostrud exercitation ullamco laboris nisi ut aliquip ex ea commodo consequat. Duis aute irure dolor in reprehenderit in voluptate velit esse cillum dolore eu fugiat nulla pariatur. Excepteur sint occaecat cupidatat non proident, sunt in culpa qui officia deserunt mollit anim id est laborum.

Lorem ipsum dolor sit amet, consectetur adipisicing elit, sed do eiusmod tempor incididunt ut labore et dolore magna aliqua. Ut enim ad minim veniam, quis nostrud exercitation

Lorem ipsum dolor sit amet, consectetur adipisicing elit, sed do eiusmod tempor incididunt ut labore et dolore magna aliqua. Ut enim ad minim veniam, quis nostrud exercitation ullamco laboris nisi ut aliquip ex ea commodo consequat. Duis aute irure dolor in reprehenderit in voluptate velit esse cillum dolore eu fugiat nulla pariatur. Excepteur sint occaecat cupidatat non proident, sunt in culpa qui officia deserunt mollit anim id est laborum.

Lorem ipsum dolor sit amet, consectetur adipisicing elit, sed do eiusmod tempor incididunt ut labore et dolore magna aliqua. Ut enim ad minim veniam, quis nostrud exercitation ullamco laboris nisi ut aliquip ex ea commodo consequat. Duis aute irure dolor in voluptate velit esse cillum dolore eu fugiat nulla pariatur. Excepteur sint occaecat cupidatat non proident, sunt in culpa qui officia deserunt mollit anim id est laborum.

Lorem ipsum dolor sit amet, consectetur adipisicing elit, sed do eiusmod tempor incididunt ut labore et dolore magna aliqua. Ut enim ad minim veniam, quis nostrud exercitation

1. Lorem ipsum dolor sit amet, consectetur adipisicing elit, sed do eiusmod tempor incididunt ut labore et dolore magna aliqua. Ut enim ad minim veniam, quis nostrud exercitation ullamco laboris nisi ut aliquip ex ea commodo consequat. Duis aute irure dolor in reprehenderit in voluptate velit

2. Lorem ipsum dolor sit amet, consectetur adipisicing elit, sed do eiusmod tempor incididunt ut labore et dolore magna aliqua. Ut enim ad minim veniam, quis nostrud exercitation ullamco laboris nisi ut aliquip ex ea commodo consequat. Duis aute irure dolor in reprehenderit in voluptate velit

Correct paragraph spacing.

It may not seem natural in family histories to use many headlines and sub-heads, but your reader will appreciate the visual break if you do.

Paragraphs

Paragraphs are the basic building block of your book, so make paragraphs look their best.

The first paragraph in a chapter or after a headline or subhead should not have an indent—all other paragraphs should.

Indents should not be created by using a tab or by spacing over. Create a style with a first line indent instead. If you turn your manuscript over to a typesetter full of extra spaces or tabs, he or she will have to remove them which will cost them time and you money.

Set your indent to one quarter of an inch (.25") and not larger unless you are using big type for the visually impaired. Unfortunately, many word processing programs have the default set to an ungainly half inch (.5").

Never use a double return to create space between paragraphs. Most of the time, you will not need extra space between paragraphs, the indent will give the reader enough of a visual break. If you want more white space on the page, create a paragraph style with slightly more space above each paragraph.

Quotes

If you transcribe a document or quote another author directly, the entire para-graph(s) should be indented from both sides to form a narrower block of text. Create a bit more space above and below quoted paragraphs, as well. Quoted paragraphs also should be fully justified (explanation below).

Justified Text

In books, paragraphs should be fully justified not justified ragged right. That is, they should look like a square block of text. In the era of typewriters, ragged right was unavoidable. The type along the right-hand edge of the page was uneven (ragged). Modern software creates much better looking fully-justified text blocks.

One potential problem with full justification is the text on the last line of each paragraph. If there are only a couple of words, full justification will spread the words out to the right-hand edge leaving unnaturally large spaces between the words. Most word processing programs give you a way to keep the last line of each fully-justified paragraph together.

Use centering and ragged right justification sparingly; in fact, almost never. Poetry with short lines can be centered, but a full paragraph that is centered is difficult to read.

Hyphenation

Most of the time, automatic hyphenation is fine because it avoids creating rivers of white down the page which disturbs the reader's ability to move smoothly

---

Justified Ragged Right

Lorem ipsum dolor sit amet, consectetur adipisicing elit, sed do eiusmod tempor incididunt ut labore et dolore magna aliqua. Ut enim ad minim veniam, quis nostrud exercitation ullamco laboris nisi ut aliquip ex ea commodo consequat. Duis aute irure

Ragged right.

Fully Justified Correctly

Lorem ipsum dolor sit amet, consectetur adipisicing elit, sed do eiusmod tempor incididunt ut labore et dolore magna aliqua. Ut enim ad minim veniam, quis nostrud exercitation ullamco laboris nisi ut aliquip ex ea commodo consequat.

Fully Justified Incorrectly

Lorem ipsum dolor sit amet, consectetur adipisicing elit, sed do eiusmod tempor incididunt ut labore et dolore magna aliqua. Ut enim ad minim veniam, quis nostrud exercitation ullamco laboris nisi ut aliquip ex ea commodo consequat.

Fully justified correctly (left); Fully justified incorrectly (forced outward spacing) (right).

from left to right, word to word. On occasion, automatic hyphenation will result in line after line of hyphens stacked on top of each other. If this happens, you can artificially hyphenate a few words to make the paragraph look better.

Watch for odd hyphenation breaks. You would not want menswear to become men-swear, or therapist to become the-rapist.

Widows and Orphans

Widows and orphans are bits of text that do not fit neatly into the column grid.

Widows are created when: the last line of a paragraph appears on the following page or at the top of the next column; a headline or subhead is in one column (page) but the paragraph that follows it is in another column (page); or the last bullet in a list is in another column (page).

Page layout programs have much better tools to control widows and orphans than do word processors, including ways to control white space and hyphenation, commands to keep lines together, and the ability to alter the length of a column to force a line into the next column.

If you are using a word processor, one way to control widows is to add a hard return before a widowed headline to force it into the next column or onto the next

6   Book Title

Lorem ipsum dolor sit amet, consectetur adipisicing elit, sed do eiusmod tempor incididunt ut labore et dolore magna aliqua. Ut enim ad minim veniam, quis nostrud exercitation ullamco laboris nisi ut aliquip ex ea commodo consequat. Duis aute irure dolor in reprehenderit in voluptate velit esse cillum dolore eu fugiat nulla pariatur. Excepteur sint occaecat cupidatat non proident, sunt in culpa qui officia deserunt mollit anim id laborum.

Lorem ipsum dolor sit amet, consectetur adipisicing elit, sed do eiusmod tempor incididunt ut labore et dolore magna aliqua. Ut enim ad minim veniam, quis nostrud exercitation ullamco laboris nisi ut aliquip ex ea commodo consequat. Duis aute irure dolor in reprehenderit in voluptate velit esse cillum dolore eu fugiat nulla pariatur. Excepteur sint occaecat cupidatat non proident, sunt in culpa qui officia deserunt mollit anim id est laborum.

Lorem ipsum dolor sit amet, consectetur adipisicing elit, sed do eiusmod tempor incididunt ut labore et dolore magna aliqua. Ut enim ad minim veniam, quis nostrud exercitation ullamco laboris nisi ut aliquip ex ea commodo consequat. Duis aute irure dolor in reprehenderit in voluptate velit esse cillum dolore eu fugiat nulla pariatur. Excepteur sint occaecat cupidatat non proident, sunt in culpa qui officia deserunt mollit anim id est laborum.

Lorem ipsum dolor sit amet, consectetur adipisicing elit, sed do eiusmod tempor incididunt ut labore et dolore magna aliqua. Ut enim ad minim veniam, quis nostrud exercitation ullamco laboris nisi ut aliquip ex ea commodo consequat. Duis aute irure dolor in reprehenderite velit esse cillum dolore eu fugiat nulla pariatur.

Headline headline
Excepteur sint occaecat cupi-

datat non proident, sunt in.

Lorem ipsum dolor sit amet, consectetur adipisicing elit, sed do eiusmod tempor incididunt ut labore et dolore magna aliqua. Ut enim ad minim veniam, quis nostrud exercitation ullamco laboris nisi ut aliquip ex ea commodo consequat. Duis aute irure dolor in reprehenderit in voluptate velit esse cillum dolore eu fugiat nulla pariatur. Excepteur sint occaecat cupidatat non proident, sunt in culpa qui officia deserunt mollit anim id est laborum.UtLorem ipsum dolor sit amet, consectetur adipisicing elit, sed do eiusmod tempor incididunt ut labore et dolore magna aliqua. Ut enim ad minim veniam, quis nostrud exercitation ullamco laboris nisi ut aliquip ex ea commodo consequat. Duis aute irure dolor in reprehenderit in voluptate velit esse cillum dolore eu fugiat nulla pariatur. Excepteur sint occaecat cupidatat non proident.
• sunt in culpa qui officia
• deserunt mollit anim id

• est officia laborum.

Lorem ipsum dolor sit amet, consectetur adipisicing elit, sed do eiusmod tempor incididunt ut labore et dolore magna aliqua. Ut enim ad minim veniam, quis nostrud exercitation ullamco laboris nisi ut aliquip ex ea commodo consequat. Duis aute irure dolor in reprehenderit in voluptate velit esse cillum dolore eu fugiat nulla pariatur. Excepteur sint occaecat cupidatat non proident, sunt in culpa qui officia deserunt mollit anim id est laborum.

Lorem ipsum dolor sit amet, consectetur adipisicing elit, sed do eiusmod tempor incididunt ut labore et dolore magna aliqua. Ut enim ad minim veniam, quis nostrud exercitation ullamco laboris nisi ut aliquip ex ea commodo consequat. Duis aute irure dolor in reprehenderit in voluptate velit esse cillum dolore eu fugiat nulla pariatur. Excepteur sint occaecat cupidatat non proi-

apter Title   7

Widows and orphans.

page. If you have a widowed bullet or a widowed line, see if you can cut the text above without changing the meaning to allow enough space for the line or bullet to remain with the paragraph or list.

Orphans are created when: the first line of a paragraph appears in one column (page) but the rest of the paragraph appears in the next column (page); the last word of a paragraph is left on a line by itself.

One way to control orphans is to turn on or off automatic hyphenation for the paragraph. This may shift another word onto the last line of the paragraph. Another option is to alter the text without altering the meaning so there are fewer words fit in the paragraph.

Initials and Acronyms

How you handle people known only by their initials is a matter of style. In most books, there are no spaces between initials, so D.S. Yates rather than D. S. Yates.

Acronyms typically do not have periods between the letters, so NASA rather than N.A.S.A.

Some acronyms, such as AM and PM, are typically set in small caps rather than in full caps, although some style guides use a.m. and p.m. (or am and pm) instead. Small caps are a function of the font, although not all fonts have a small caps option.

How you handle initials and acronyms is a matter of preference as long as you are consistent throughout.

Web and Email Addresses

Because we are in the Internet age, your book may include website URLs (website addresses), or email addresses. In electronic books (eBooks), these addresses can be made into hyperlinks so that the reader can click on the link to be taken to the website, or to launch an email program. In printed books, it is up to you whether or not you leave the color and underlining that word processing programs add when addresses are hyperlinked. Most word processors use a bright blue for hyperlinks, which may not be as readable in print, as changing them to black would be. Increasing the letter spacing in website addresses also makes them easier to read.

Punctuation

Punctuation can make or break meaning. If you have not already read Lynne Truss's book, *Eats, Shoots & Leaves: A Zero Tolerance Approach to Punctuation*, you should. Single-handedly, she is conducting a rather hilarious war on the proliferation of commas.

Dashes and Hyphens

Hyphens are used to create compound adjectives, such as state-of-the-art computer. Hyphens are used for compound numbers (forty-four books), double last names (Sir Watkin Williams-Wynn), and spelled-out fractions (two-thirds). Hyphens once were used to distinguish all pre-fixes (pre-arranged), but less so today. If eliminating the hyphen would cause confusion with another word (recovered a lost wallet versus re-covered a sofa), then use the hyphen.

Dashes are not hyphens, nor double hyphens. Fortunately, most word processors will turn double hyphens into an em dash. Unfortunately, most word processors do not know the difference between the em dash and the en dash.

An en dash, a dash approximately the width of the letter n, is used to indicate duration, so October–December (October through December), or 10–12 (ten to twelve).

An em dash, a dash approximately the width of the letter m, is used when you want the reader to pause a bit longer than they would for a comma, but not as long as they would for a period. Em dashes are a matter of preference. Many authors will use parentheses to set off a change in thought, others prefer em dashes.

En and em dashes do not have spaces—before or after them.

Ellipses

Ellipses, a series of three periods (...) with a bit of extra space in between, are used to indicate a long pause in thought, or that material was left out of a quote.

Fortunately, if you put three periods in a row without adding a space in between, most word processors will display them correctly.

If you end a sentence with an ellipsis, you still need a period to end the sentence, so there will be four dots.

Ellipses require a full space before and a full space after.

Special Characters

Special characters include bullets, copyright symbols, and accent marks on foreign language words. These special characters are found in glyph or symbols menus. Fortunately, many word processors and page layout programs automatically insert correct accents on common words such as cliché.

Serial Commas

Although Lynne Truss is waging an admirable war on the proliferation of commas, sometimes the serial comma is needed when listing items. For example, you could eliminate the last comma from a list such as bananas, oranges, and apples. If however, you eliminated the last comma from, "To my siblings, Mom, and Grandma," you would be implying that your mother and grandmother were your siblings (i.e. "To my siblings, Mom and Grandma").

It is up to you how you handle serial commas, as long as meaning is clear.

Quotation Marks

Quotation marks are not apostrophes. Quotation marks are the curly-cue-looking marks that face one way at the beginning of a quote, and the other way at the end. Make this simple on yourself by turning on the "smart quotes," in your word processing or page layout program and avoid fonts that do not have true, left and right quotation marks.

Quotation marks should not be used for emphasis. Use italics if you want to get the reader's attention. Use quotation marks for direct quotations, to alert readers that a term is being used in a non-standard way such as for irony or sarcasm, or to replace the words "so-called."

Place commas and periods inside quotation marks. Colons and semi-colons belong outside quotation marks. Place question marks or exclamation points inside if they belong to quoted material, otherwise outside.

Semi-Colons

Semi-colons are used to link two independent clauses together. Most of the time, however, you can use a period and start a new sentence with the same effect.

You can also use a semi-colon to link items in a list together where a comma could cause confusion. For example, "some people choose to go places by motorized vehicles, cars, motorcycles or busses; but others, for different reasons, choose to walk, bicycle or roller skate."

Apostrophes

Apostrophes are used to indicate possession (e.g. John's book), to create contractions (e.g. don't) and to indicate the omission of letters, so Rock and Roll becomes Rock 'n' Roll because both the "a" and the "d" in "and" are replaced with an apostrophe.

A single, straight apostrophe indicates feet (e.g. 125'). A double, straight apostrophe indicates inches (e.g. 3").

In the 80s, means the temperature is in the 80s. In the '80s, means the decade of the 1980s (or 1880s). There is no apostrophe when referring to a decade (1850s) unless you are indicating possession (1850's clothing styles).

Lines, Rules and Strokes

The terms lines, rules and strokes all mean a line. Most often lines are used in the header to separate the book title or chapter title from the body text.

If you use lines, choose a numbered point size for the thickness of your lines. Avoid the hairline setting, because "hairline" is interpreted differently by each printer's machinery, so the results may be unexpected.

Color

If the interior of your book is color throughout, you can use color for headlines and subheads to make them stand out. Black text is still the easiest to read, so if you use a color for headlines or subheads, choose one that is dark enough to be read easily, and use the same color throughout the book for consistency. Any dark color can work, although people with red-green color blindness will appreciate it if you avoid those two colors.

Cross References

You may need to include cross references to chapters, numbered sections, illustrations or pages. The only way to create cross references without creating a lot of extra work for yourself, is to leave a visual indicator in the text (e.g. [XXXXX]), and wait until the final page proofs are available before adding the appropriate reference.

Most family histories do not need cross references except in the index. You can accomplish much of the same with good explanations in foot- or endnotes.

Clean Up Your Manuscript Files

Before you begin typesetting (applying styles to the text), clean up your manuscript files.

One common habit of people who learned to type on typewriters is to put two spaces before the beginning of a new sentence. Modern word processors use proportional spacing at the end of sentences so they do not need the extra space. Use the Find/Replace command to search for two spaces and replace them with a single space. Repeat this task until the software indicates that no more replacements have been made. This will eliminate the extra spaces created by the old typewriter trick of spacing over instead of using tabs, as well.

Remove extra tabs. Paragraphs should not be created by tabbing over. They should be given a style with a first line indent instead (see Creating Styles below).

Eliminate double returns using Find/Replace as well. Paragraphs should not be separated by double returns. The first line indent in the next paragraph will be enough to distinguish when one paragraph ends and the next begins.

Extra space is used to indicate the start of a new section or a change in topic where a new chapter or headline is not necessary. Double returns are not used to create this extra space, either. Instead, create a paragraph style to govern this situation, with even more above the paragraph than that above a subhead, but less than a double return.

Look for odd line breaks or out of place page breaks, and missing punctuation.

Once your manuscript is clean, you can begin creating styles to govern how the text will look.

Create Styles

Most word processing and page layout programs allow you to create styles for different types of text (paragraphs, headlines and so on), and then apply the style when appropriate.

The easiest way to start formatting an entire chapter is to create a style for the majority of the body copy and apply it to the entire chapter. Then you can create new styles for first paragraphs that do not have indents, headlines that could be in bigger or bolder text than the body, and image captions that should be somewhat smaller than the body text.

In most software, each time you encounter a need for a new style, you can manually format the text, then select that text to create a new style—the software will copy each of the attributes of the new text into the new style. After the new style is created, simply highlight the text and apply the new style when needed.

Good typesetting makes your manuscript easy to read. Choosing appropriate fonts and type sizes, spacing between letters and lines, and justifying body text are the heart and soul of the typesetting rules. If you can also avoid common punctuation errors, and eliminate any widows and orphans, your book's interior will look like it was typeset by a professional.

Front Matter

This section will take you through the front matter in order of how the front matter should appear in your book, from the first item (the endsheets) to the last item (the introduction).

Almost every front matter part mentioned here, should begin on a right-hand (recto) page which means that there may be blank pages within your front matter. Beginning each new section on a right-hand page is a publishing convention—a tradition, but in the interest of saving space, many publishers today are running each successive part on the next available page.

There are not many examples in this section because you will find working examples in the front matter of this book.

Endsheets

In hard cover books, endsheets are used to reinforce the attachment from the cloth cover to the sewn-together pages of the interior, so you will find an endsheet in the front and the back of the book. If you are using an offset printer, you may be able to choose the illustration or design for your endsheets. Other printers have stock designs for you to choose from, although many use a common endsheet.

Endsheets are not necessary to hold the covers onto softbound (paperback) books, therefore, are not used. With some printers, it is possible to print an illustration on the inside cover of a paperback book, but it is almost always an extra charge. Most print-on-demand printers do not offer this option.

Frontispiece

A frontispiece is an illustration on the left-hand (verso) side facing the title page. These are common, mostly in high-end coffee table books.

Although an illustration could go on the reverse side of the endsheet, a frontispiece is usually a separate page using the same paper as the interior, rather than the heavier endsheet paper.

Endorsements or Blurbs

Endorsements are also called blurbs. It is common with commercially-available books to solicit short blurbs from well-known authors or experts. The best ones belong on the cover or dust jacket flaps. Any others go on pages before the half-title page, and these pages are not numbered.

It is uncommon for family histories to include blurbs, but if you are going to solicit them, five or six will do. Keep them short and sweet. If you are soliciting a well-known author, expert, or member of your family, offer a blurb already written for his or her approval or to edit as he or she sees fit.

Blurbs are typically set in the main body font, in quotes. The name of the blurb's author follows on a separate line either centered or flush right, followed by a line containing any titles, awards or books he or she has written, also centered or flush right. Use italics for book titles.

Half-Title Page

A half-title page was used more than a century ago to identify an unsold book. In those days, books were printed, but not bound until sold, so that the new owner could choose the binding. Today, half title pages are not necessary but if you include one, the reverse side should be blank.

The half-title page should be typeset in whatever font you have chosen for your chapter headers but big enough to make a statement, placed about one third of the way down the page.

Ad Card

One option for the reverse side of the title page is to include an ad card—a list of other books you have written. Look at the ad card in this book. It begins with: "Other books by the author" and lists the titles. You could begin with: "Author of ..." or "Also by ..."

The ad card is typeset in the main body font, flush left, but justified ragged right. If you will only be listing titles, full justification may stretch the words apart unnaturally.

Title Page

Typeset the title in the same font and size as the half-title page, and place it about one third of the way down the page. The title should be followed by the subtitle in the same font but smaller. The author's name should be placed about two thirds of the way down the page, followed by the publishing company, and the city where the book was published (the city of the publishing company not the printer) at the bottom. If you have a logo for your publishing company, it can go on this page, as well.

The reverse side of the title page is the copyrights page.

Copyrights Page

The copyrights page belongs on the back of the title page and should include:

- The title and subtitle
- The author's name
- The publisher's name and physical address
- A copyright notice (the symbol and year)
- The name of the copyright owner
- The expression "all rights reserved" to give you the maximum protection in case of copyright infringement
- A disclaimer, if needed. Most books today include one even if not needed.

- Publishing history (edition or print run if there has been more than one)
- Printed in the United States of America (wherever the book was printed)

If you plan to sell your book commercially or to libraries, also consider:

Library of Congress (LOC) Catalog in Publication Data [LCC CIP]. The CIP data is bibliographic data prepared by the Library of Congress to help libraries and book dealers correctly catalog the book.

Before the book is published, apply for the CIP Program online (www.loc.gov/publish/cip/).

You can also create your own CIP data, called the Publisher's CIP data, if you do not want to wait months for the Library of Congress to do this for you.

Library of Congress Catalog Number (LCCN or PCN—Preassigned Control Number). A Library of Congress catalog control number (or preassigned number) is a unique identification number given by the LOC, that is included in their national database available to libraries, book stores and other commercial suppliers. Before your book is published, apply for a Library of Congress PCN (www.loc.gov/publish/pcn/).

International Standard Book Number (ISBN). An ISBN is like the Social Security number for you book. It is a unique number assigned by the U.S. ISBN Agency run by the Bowker Company (www.isbn.org). From the website, you can purchase a single ISBN, a block of ten, a block of 100, and so on. A single ISBN costs $125.00. A block of ten costs $295.00.

If you are planning to publish through a print-on-demand printer, many offer ISBNs free of charge. The only drawback to using one of your printer's ISBNs is that the printer becomes the publisher of record, and not you or your publishing company. For many family history authors, however, using the printer's free ISBN is the simplest way to go.

The copyrights page should be typeset in the main body font, but the majority of the text will be set at a point size small enough to fit all of the above information onto one page. Use the copyrights page of this book as a guide.

Dedication

Many authors use the dedication page to thank whoever has been the greatest influence while writing the book. Most dedications are short. Longer tributes belong in the acknowledgments section.

The dedication page should be typeset in main body font, in Roman (plain) text or italics.

Dedication pages are optional. If used, they should occupy a right-hand page, and the back should be blank.

Acknowledgments

Acknowledgments are your opportunity to thank the people who helped you research and write the book. Acknowledgments are optional.

If used, be rigorous when checking the spelling of each person's name, and if they have a title, use the correct, most recently earned title.

Acknowledgments begin on a right-hand page, and can be placed after the dedication, after the preface, within the preface, or in the back matter. If your acknowledgments run an odd number of pages, the last page should be blank.

Acknowledgments should be typeset in the main body font, and if there are many paragraphs, should follow the rules for the rest of the book. If there is a single paragraph, it can be set in italics about one third of the way down the page.

Epigraph

An epigraph is a pertinent quote that sets the tone for the book, and is optional. Epigraphs are sometimes used on the first page of each chapter.

If the epigraph is typeset on a right-hand page, the back of the page should be blank. Epigraphs can also go on the left-hand page facing the table of contents, if that page is blank.

Epigraphs should be in quotes, in the main body font, in Roman (plain) text or italics. The author's name (or anonymous, if not known) should be placed on a line beneath the quote, followed by the source of the quote on another line. If the source is a book title, it should be typeset in italics.

Table of Contents

The table of contents (TOC) begins on a right-hand page. If there is only one page, the reverse side should be left blank. If the contents run more than one page, they are called contents *only* and can be set *either* on a left-right, two-page spread (pages ii and iii, for example), or beginning on a right-hand page with the remainder on the next left-hand page (pages iii and iv, in this case).

The table of contents can be set in either the main body font or the font

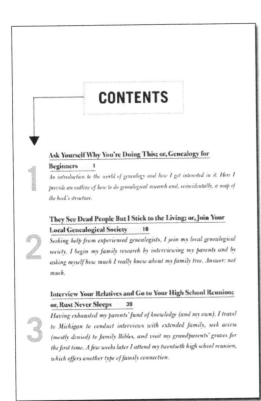

Table of Contents.

you have chosen for your headlines and subheads. The page numbers should be typeset with a right-aligned tab to keep the right-hand edges of the page numbers even down the page.

The table of contents should show the number of the first page of each part of the front matter, the parts (or sections), each chapter, the back matter and the index. How much else you include beyond the chapter number, is up to you. You could include the chapter title (if there are chapter titles), and a running list of subtitles to give the reader an idea of what to expect in each chapter. The example (previous page) from Buzzy Jackson's book *Shaking the Family Tree* uses a running narrative to give readers an idea of what is included in each chapter.

Illustrations

If your book has many illustrations, include a list of illustrations (also called a list of figures). If the illustrations correspond closely with the text, the list is probably not necessary because the information will be provided in the captions, descriptive text or footnotes.

A list of illustrations should include the name (or a description) of the illustration, plus the page number where it occurs. The page numbers should be typeset with a right-aligned tab to keep the right-hand edges of the page numbers even down the page. The back side of a list of illustrations should be blank.

Tables

Lists of tables are common in scientific literature and occasionally in military histories but are uncommon in family histories. If you need one, the back of the page should be left blank. A list of tables should be typeset in the same way as a list of illustrations.

Foreword

A foreword is statement about the book written by someone other than the author. Forewords are common in biographies of famous people, but not common in family histories.

If, for example, you have a famous ancestor and want to include a foreword by an expert, then by all means do so. A foreword longer than two to three pages should have a title of its own with the author's name at the beginning, rather than at the end, which is typical for short forewords.

The foreword should be typeset in the main body text and follow the same rules as the body as far as paragraphs, headlines and subheads. If your foreword runs an odd number of pages, the next page should be left blank so that the next section will begin on a right-hand page.

Typeset the following using the same rules as the foreword:

Front Matter	**Body**	**Back Matter**
Preface	Epilogue	Postscript
Methods	Afterword	About the Author
Contributors		Glossary
Chronology		Colophon
Characters		
Permissions		
Prologue		

Preface

A preface is optional. It is a way for you, the author, to talk directly to the reader. A preface is one place to explain your research methods, the reasons you undertook this project, or why you are so interested in this family. Many authors include their acknowledgments in the preface. If you do, there is no need for another section of acknowledgments elsewhere.

Methods

A methods section (also called editorial method) is used in scholarly works where the author's analysis needs explanation. In a family history, you may want to alert readers to how you arrived at a conclusion if the explanation is important before they begin reading.

You could explain why, for example, you have modernized the spelling and capitalization from a diary entry to make it more readable, if you used a common spelling for a surname to keep family lines straight, or anglicized unfamiliar foreign words. Much of this could be included in footnotes or endnotes rather than in the front matter.

Contributors

A list of contributors is optional. If someone provided expertise that calls for more than a simple acknowledgment, a list of contributors is the place to give credit along with a short explanation describing how each person or group helped you with this project.

Chronology

A chronology can be helpful if the order of events is not clear, as may happen in a collection of letters, or in a diary with missing entries.

Use a chronology to provide a broader historical context. For example, a list of events preceding the U.S. involvement in the Mexican War and the battles that took place thereafter may be helpful because readers may not be well acquainted with the events of the Mexican War.

A chronology can also serve as a quick reference if your book covers multiple families or time lines.

A chronology should begin on a right-hand page, unless it would be simpler for the reader to use a left-right spread.

Characters

Occasionally in fiction you may find a list of characters. In a family history, you could use a genealogical chart to show relationships instead.

A list of characters could include: every member of the family; ancestors who are not written about in this book but who are known; and people outside the family if they play an important role somewhere in the story, such as business partners, neighbors, or other members of a military unit.

Alphabetize by last name followed by a comma and the first name. To help readers keep people with similar names straight, include birth and death dates as well as a short descriptive paragraph about the character. Typeset the names in bold or italics either as subheads or run-in subheads.

Permissions

If you have only a few places where you need to acknowledge permissions given to use material for the book, they could be placed in a footnote, an endnote, an image credit or a side bar. A list may be easier if you have many permissions to acknowledge.

A list of permissions can be placed in either the front or the back matter and should begin on a right-hand page. You can organize the list of permissions in order as the items occur, or alphabetically by repository to avoid repeating information if many items came from one repository. When describing sources, give the location in the book by chapter and (or) page, then use the same style as endnotes or footnotes, typically using either *Evidence Explained* or *The Chicago Manual of Style*.

Prologue

A prologue is used in fiction to set the scene for the story and is told in the voice of one of the characters rather than the author's. If you want to set the scene for your readers this way, there is no reason you should not.

Second Half-Title Page

If the front matter is long, you can use a second half-title page to give readers a visual clue where the body of the book begins. The second half-title page should look exactly like the first half-title page.

Introduction

Use an introduction to set the stage. Explain your purpose or goals in writing the book. Give the reader historical context or to make clear the organization and scope of the book. Explain what the book will not do, for example, if you have limited the scope to a specific family or to individuals within the family.

The introduction, although technically a part of the front matter, is the beginning of the book. The introduction should follow the typesetting rules for the body, with one exception. Although the page numbers in the preceding front matter sections are set in lowercase Roman numerals, switch to Arabic numerals when you begin the introduction.

Some publishers will continue the page numbers from the front matter, so if the last page of the front matter was page viii, then the first page of the introduction would be page 9. Others will restart the numbering with page 1 on the first page of the introduction. The first style is more traditional, although the latter style is becoming more common.

Much of what can be included in the front matter is optional. The sections that *are* necessary are the title page, the copyrights page, and the table of contents. Beyond that, it is up to you as the publisher to decide what else to include.

The Body

Most of the typesetting for the body of the book is about the paragraphs, headlines and subheads covered in the previous section. The remainder is how to create first pages different enough to give the reader a visual clue that a new section or chapter is beginning.

Parts or Sections—First Pages

If you have divided the manuscript into parts or sections, you will need an opening page for each. These pages should act as dividers and should be right-hand pages with the reverse side left blank unless you wish to use an epigraph or illustration there.

Typeset the part or section title in large letters about one third of the way down the page using the same font as your title and subtitle. You can use the part or section title alone, or include a mini-table of contents for the section.

Neither the front nor the back of this page should have a running header or a page number, but these pages contribute to the page count. So even though they should not have page numbers on them, count the pages following a part or section divider as if they did.

Chapters—First Pages

The first page of each chapter should be easy to find while thumbing through a book. Traditionally, chapters begin on a new page on the right-hand side. If you end up with many blank pages because chapters have an uneven number of pages, you can ignore the convention to minimize the number of blank pages—with two exceptions: chapters *must* begin on a *new* page (whether left or right) and Chapter One *must* begin on a *right-hand* page.

Chapter titles are optional but numbers are not. If you use titles, they should be consistent in tone from one chapter to the next. In other words, do not use a whimsical title for one, and a serious statement for the next.

Chapter numbers start at one and are consecutive no matter what section they are in. In other words, chapter numbers are never repeated.

The first page of a chapter should not have a page number or a running header. The chapter number and (or) title should begin at least two inches from the top of the page, but could be as low as one third of the way down the page with the body text beginning about half-way down the page.

Footnotes or Endnotes

Whether you put your source citations in footnotes or endnotes is up to you. Opinions are divided about whether readers would rather refer back to an endnotes page or read footnotes as they occur in the text.

Section II

Mary James
(1849–1902)

and

John Nathaniel Hammet
(1844–1900)

Section 2

Mary James (1849-1902)

and

John Nathaniel Hammet (1844-1900)

Chapter 8: Luella Ann Hammet
Chapter 9: James William Hammet
Chapter 10: Corrinne Sophie Hammet
Chapter 11: Mary Louisiana Hammet
Chapter 13: Winston George Hammet
Chapter 14: Nelson Grant Hammet

Section divider with number and title (left); Section divider with mini-table of contents (right).

If you use footnotes, leave enough room between the text and the footnote to make it obvious, or use a rule (line) in between. Most word processing and page layout programs create footnotes for you, so they are not technically footers because they will change from page to page depending upon how many notes there are on each page.

If you use endnotes, place them either at the end of the chapter, or together in the back matter.

Typical formatting for footnotes or endnotes is as follows:

1. Author (first then last), *Title in Italics* (City of publication: Publisher, date), p. number.

Epilogue

An epilogue is a final note from you, the author, or as a continuation of the main narrative to bring closure to the book.

Afterword

An afterword, is a way for you, the author, to give your final thoughts. Set the book into a larger context within the family, let readers know about additional research you are doing, tell a funny story that wraps up the book, or give the reader an enticing preview of your next book.

Chapter 4

Lorem ipsum dolor sit amet, consectetur adipisicing elit, sed do eiusmod tempor incididunt ut labore et dolore magna aliqua. Ut enim ad minim veniam, quis nostrud exercitation ullamco laboris nisi ut aliquip ex ea commodo consequat. Duis aute irure dolor in reprehenderit in voluptate velit esse cillum dolore eu fugiat nulla pariatur. Excepteur sint occaecat cupidatat non proident, sunt in culpa qui officia deserunt mollit anim id est laborum.

Lorem ipsum dolor sit amet, consectetur adipisicing elit, sed do eiusmod tempor incididunt ut labore et dolore magna aliqua. Ut enim ad minim veniam, quis nostrud exercitation ullamco laboris nisi ut aliquip ex ea commodo consequat. Duis aute irure dolor in reprehenderit in voluptate velit esse cillum dolore eu fugiat nulla pariatur. Excepteur sint occaecat cupidatat non proident, sunt in culpa qui officia deserunt mollit anim id est laborum.

Lorem ipsum dolor sit amet, consectetur adipisicing elit, sed do eiusmod tempor incididunt ut labore et dolore magna aliqua. Ut enim ad minim veniam, quis nostrud exercitation

---

Chapter 4

The Westward Migration Begins

Lorem ipsum dolor sit amet, consectetur adipisicing elit, sed do eiusmod tempor incididunt ut labore et dolore magna aliqua. Ut enim ad minim veniam, quis nostrud exercitation ullamco laboris nisi ut aliquip ex ea commodo consequat. Duis aute irure dolor in reprehenderit in voluptate velit esse cillum dolore eu fugiat nulla pariatur. Excepteur sint occaecat cupidatat non proident, sunt in culpa qui officia deserunt mollit anim id est laborum.

Lorem ipsum dolor sit amet, consectetur adipisicing elit, sed do eiusmod tempor incididunt ut labore et dolore magna aliqua. Ut enim ad minim veniam, quis nostrud exercitation ullamco laboris nisi ut aliquip ex ea commodo consequat. Duis aute irure dolor in reprehenderit in voluptate velit esse cillum dolore eu fugiat nulla pariatur. Excepteur sint occaecat cupidatat non proident, sunt in culpa qui officia deserunt mollit anim id est laborum.

Lorem ipsum dolor sit amet, consectetur adipisicing elit, sed do eiusmod tempor incididunt ut labore et dolore magna aliqua. Ut enim ad minim veniam, quis nostrud exercitation ullamco laboris nisi ut aliquip ex ea commodo consequat. Duis aute irure dolor in reprehenderit in voluptate velit esse cillum dolore eu fugiat

---

Chapter with number (left); Chapter with number and title (right).

Conclusion

If you did not do so in the epilogue, use the conclusion to provide a brief summary of the main points.

Because most of the typesetting for the book concerns paragraphs, headlines, subheads and running headers, what is left is to create visual breaks for parts (sections) and the first page of each chapter, and to decide where to place the source citations—in footnotes or endnotes.

Back Matter

The back matter begins when the stories cease and you have had your last word as the author—well, almost. There is the possibility of a postscript. Back matter typically includes appendices, endnotes, a bibliography and an index. Your back matter could also include a postscript, an about the author section, a glossary, errata, a colophon, an excerpt from another book, and an order form.

The following front matter content can be placed in the back matter if you prefer, including the: acknowledgments, lists of illustrations, tables, contributors, and permissions.

Postscript

A postscript is a place to add something you were unable to include in the book. If you came across additional research, for example, give a brief synopsis.

About the Author

An about the author section is optional. It is an opportunity to tell the reader who you are and why you wrote the book. It should include a brief biography and a photograph is customary. Often, a brief version of this is placed on the back cover, or a longer version on the dust jacket of a hardcover edition.

Appendices

Items in an appendix may explain, elaborate or clarify information that did not fit neatly into the narrative.

The following examples are material that may not fit neatly into the narrative:

- A complete list of names from a military unit
- A list of which people are buried in which cemetery
- A complete transcription of a document mentioned in the text
- Information, documents or photographs gathered too late to be included elsewhere
- Any difficult-to-find items mentioned in the book (reproduction pieces available by catalog or collector's website, for example)

Each appendix needs a title, a number or a letter. The first appendix should appear on a right-hand page. Each subsequent appendix could begin on the next available page, right or left, to avoid blank pages.

Addendum

An addendum is a section of new material that was unavailable when the book was written. Often, an addendum is added in a subsequent edition, updating information without a complete re-write.

Glossary

A glossary is optional, but appreciated if you use: many foreign words; jargon or technical phrases (common if you are describing a process or a profession from a century or more ago); words used during the era of your ancestors but out of use today; or unfamiliar slang (e.g. military slang).

Alphabetize glossary terms followed by a brief explanation.

Endnotes

If you want to place endnotes in the back matter, they should begin on a right-hand page, be organized by chapter, then by note number. Leave extra space before the start of each chapter's endnotes to create a visual break.

Bibliography

While a formal bibliography is optional in a family history, readers may be interested in what books and articles you consulted in addition to any original source material you used.

You will find standard bibliographic style guides for published materials in *The Elements of Style* by William Strunk and E.B. White, or *A Manual for Writers of Term Papers, Theses, and Dissertations* by Kate L. Turabian.

Your bibliography could be organized by family, location, research facility or topic. If you organize in a way other than alphabetical by author's last name for the whole list, use a subhead to indicate the start of a new section, alphabetize within the section, and leave space before the subhead as a visual break.

Index

All non-fiction books must have an index. Fortunately, most word processing and page layout software makes it possible to create index tags electronically within the body text, which are compiled into an index once the final layout is finished. It is important to compile the index last, however, to make certain text has not shifted from one page to the next during any final editing or touch ups to the layout.

Unfortunately, there is not one single set of rules for creating an index. Most publishing houses have their own criteria, as do professional indexers. As the publisher, you have a great deal of latitude in what you will include.

Indexing takes time and adds pages to the book, but, first and foremost, it should be a useful tool. Be careful not to let the task of indexing determine the contents. It is not uncommon to find books where material in the beginning is over-indexed, and material at the end is under-indexed because the indexer tired of the process.

There are three types of index listings to consider: names, places and subjects.

Every person mentioned should be included in the index. A full-name index has become the standard for genealogical works thanks to the persistence of genealogists such as Birdie Holsclaw. Your index should adhere to this standard. Besides, it is the first place your family members will look, to see where they are mentioned.

Indexing places is helpful to other people researching the area, even if they are not researching your family. If you have done a great job describing the history of a town, or what a place looked like when your ancestors lived there, another researcher may benefit from your hard work. Who knows, you may find yourself quoted or footnoted in another author's work.

Indexing subjects is a little trickier because it is hard to know what subjects are the most important to include. If you have spent time talking about battles, or the details of a profession, or have discussed the manufacturer of your grandmother's bone china, those are the kinds of subjects worth including.

An index is not merely a list of names and places, it is a way for people to retrieve information quickly, so any subject you think would help the reader find what they are looking for will be appreciated.

Index the whole book—everything from the dedication to the appendices—with a couple of exceptions. There is no need to index the colophon or copyrights page, nor the bibliography because it is already alphabetical by author's name and therefore easy to search. Endnotes or footnotes may be a different matter, if you have included other explanatory material in the note. If there are relevant entries in the explanatory material, then index it.

Basic Index Formatting. The index should begin on a right-hand page and be typeset in the body font, one or two points smaller. Each page should have a running header and page numbers, the same as the rest of the book. Use hanging indents to keep the alphabetical first letter flush left, but the remainder of the listing along with the page numbers, indented about one quarter of an inch. Use a slightly larger space between listings than the line leading for wrapped text to create a visual break or to add a bit of white space to the page. When you begin a new letter in your alphabetical list, use a subhead in bold that is slightly larger than the index body text.

Some publishers use bold page numbers to indicate illustrations, and bold italicized page numbers to indicate boxed text or tables. If you have created a list of illustrations or tables in the front matter, there is no need for this type of formatting in your index.

Page numbers are formatted according to long-standing tradition. Information that occurs on sequential pages is formatted with an en dash in between the numbers, but only if the discussion of the subject is continuous across those pages. For example, a person may be mentioned on page 140 and again on page 141, but there is *not* a continuous discussion of this person, so the formatting would be 140, 141. If there had been a continuous discussion of that person, the formatting would be 140-141. This is a subtle difference and not absolutely crucial. Most software-generated indexes will create a list of numbers separated by commas. You can save space in the index by combining a long list of consecutive page numbers (140, 141, 142, 143, 144), into a shorter run of 140-144. Whether you follow the long-standing convention of using the en dash only to indicate a continuous discussion of the subject, is up to you, although using the en dashes correctly is more accurate.

In a family history, there may be chapters where the same individual is mentioned on every page throughout a chapter. Another way to cut down on the number of times an individual is indexed, is to give the reader the first page plus a symbol (e.g. * or # or +) on which a major player is mentioned in a chapter, but no subsequent page numbers. If you shorten the number of listings this way, explain it at the beginning of the index—true of any deviation from convention—so that the reader knows what to expect.

There is no need to indicate how many times an individual is listed on a single page. An index points the reader to the page, it does not absolve the reader of reading what is there.

Formatting Subjects. Main subjects should be flush left, then broken down into minor subjects. The minor subjects should be indented a quarter of an inch using a hanging indent so that any wrapping page numbers fall at half an inch. Main subjects are capitalized, minor subjects are not unless they begin with a proper noun. If you include a cross reference, the word "see" should be in italics before the cross reference subject. Here is an example:

Wagon
    Conestoga   33, 70, 104
    repair, *see* wainwright
    trains 21-24, 47

Formatting Place Names. Formatting place names can be tricky if the place is known by more than one name during different time periods. The New Netherlands is a good example. If your ancestors lived in the Manhattan area during the Dutch rule, they would have lived in New Netherlands, not New York. If you are unsure whether your readers will be acquainted well enough with the location to know that New Netherlands became New York, you may want to include a cross reference.

New Netherlands, *see also* New York.

Another way to deal with place names where the location is the same but the name is not, is to include an explanation, such as:

Denver, Denver County (then Arapahoe County), Colorado
Denver, Arapahoe County (now Denver County), Colorado

If you have abbreviated terms within the text, use the same abbreviations in your index to maintain consistency.

Index geographic names the way a reader would look for them, so:

The Dalles, Oregon.
> The Dalles, Oregon, not Dalles, The, Oregon because "The Dalles" is recognized as the place name.

Elms, The.
> However, if you have a property name such as The Elms, it would be indexed as Elms, The and not The Elms. (Indexing can be tricky.)

Florence, Italy.
> Florence not Firenze (for an English-speaking audience)

Pear Cottage.
> Pear Cottage, not Cottage, Pear

If you use abbreviations in your place names, do so consistently, such as:
> St. Louis or Saint Louis, but not a mixture of the two
> Ste. Genevieve County for Sainte Genevieve County

Or:
> Ste. Genevieve Co. (if you also consistently abbreviate county using Co.)

Formatting People's Names. Surnames are not universal and they can be inconsistent over time which makes them tricky to index if you have included people whose families are the same but whose surnames are different. In general, whatever rule you followed for the text, repeat in the index, except where alphabetizing by your software becomes a problem. Not all software alphabetizes the same way. Microsoft Word, for example, will treat De la Rosa differently than de la Rosa, giving priority to the capitalized version. The index will show both versions but the capitalized version will come first.

Most software will treat names with spaces in them differently than names without, so these words would be alphabetized as:

De la Rosa
Deify
Delarosa
Detrimental
Di Larosa

If the number of listings between the two versions of De la Rosa is substantial, use a cross reference (e.g. *see* Di Larosa or *see* Du Larosa) so that the reader knows to look for another spelling. A different way to deal with this is to explain at the start of the index that you have made all versions of Vandergard (Vander Gard, Van Der Gard, van der Gard) the same for the purposes of indexing only.

If there are people with the same name, do something to distinguish them in the index, for example:

Josiah Smith (1830-1899)   33, 89, 90
Josiah Smith (1864-1919)   60, 71, 90
Josiah Smith (1880-1956)   78, 91, 106

Or:

Josiah Smith (the elder)   33, 89, 90
Josiah Smith (the baker)   60, 71, 90
Josiah Smith (the son)   78, 91, 106

It is natural in a family history to have many people listed with the same surname, so you will list the surname once, flush left, then alphabetize the first names indented one quarter of an inch (.25") with the hanging indent leaving any wrapping page numbers indented one half inch (.5"). For example:

Foster
   Allen 71, 77
   Bruce 50
   Carter 44

If you have a long list of people under the same surname, when you reach the next column or page, repeat the surname followed by (cont.).

Foster (cont.)
   Wesley   100
   William, Jr.   110
   William, Sr.   107

Women's names can be problematic because in order to create the most useful index, you need to refer to women by both their maiden and married names, if appropriate, and on occasion, by multiple married names. The following are examples of how to handle this.

If a woman's name was Mary Jane Jones Rankin Scarborough meaning she was born as Mary Jane Jones, married a Rankin and subsequently married a Scarborough, she should be listed as:

Jones, Mary Jane (*see* Rankin, Mary Jane, *see* Scarborough, Mary Jane)
Rankin, Mary Jane (Jones)
Scarborough, Mary Jane (Jones) (Rankin)

People with hyphenated surnames should be listed under both names as well. For example:

Gowan-Saroyan, Jane (*see* Saroyan, Jane Gowan)

If there are women who are referred to by *only* their married names, they should be listed as:

Brice, William (Mrs.)—not, Brice, Mrs. William.

If there were many women named Mrs. Brice, for example, they would all alphabetize under Brice, M (for Mrs.) and not under the letter of their husband's first name where they should.

Incorrect:
Brice, Keith
Brice, Mrs. Adam
Brice, Mrs. Bruce
Brice, Mrs. William
Brice, Nathan

Correct:
Brice, Adam (Mrs.)
Brice, Bruce (Mrs.)
Brice, Keith
Brice, Nathan
Brice, William (Mrs.)

The use of titles such as Miss and Dr. is a matter of preference in the index, unless Miss Shaw or Dr. Reynolds is the only name you have for those individuals. If you have only a last name and a title, then the titles belong in the index.

In a transcription, using a name as you find it is proper; in an index, not necessarily. For example, if you find the name Daniel, Dan'l and Dan in the body text, in the index, you may not wish to have three listings for the same person under each of these iterations. If it is clear that you are referring to the same person, use the best, most complete name—Daniel.

If there are people who are referred to by only one name, or by none at all, include whatever you need to, to reference that individual, such as:

Horace (the watchmaker)

Negro girl (b. ca 1850)

Susannah (the neighbor)

The same goes if you have a surname but no first name, for example:

Halford (cotton buyer)

Rosenkranz, Miss (housekeeper)

Surry, Miss (teacher)

Tarbox, Mr. (land agent)

If you have people who used a nickname that does not suggest their formal name, then use a cross-reference, such as: Rogers, Buzz (*see* Rogers, Alden).

Formatting Institutional Names. Formal names should be indexed as they are presented, so:

All Saints Cathedral

Miss Porter's School

Van Pelt Cemetery

These places could also be indexed under subject headings, such as:

Cemeteries

Van Pelt Cemetery

Churches

All Saints Cathedral

Schools

Miss Porter's School

Just like people with the same name, institutions with the same name should include a way to differentiate one place from the next, so:

Old Burying Ground (Boston, MA)

Old Burying Ground (Waverly, NH)

Institutions using people's names can be tricky, as well. For the most part they should be indexed as written, so either:

Harrison Trimble High School

Or:

Trimble, Harrison. *See also* Harrison Trimble High School

But not:

Trimble, Harrison (High School)

In the 19th Century, it was common for people to name their businesses after themselves. The best way to list them is both as they appear *and* by the founder's last name, for example:

C. Madison & Co.

Madison, Charles. *See also* C. Madison and Co.

Madison (C. Madison & Co.)

Index legal cases the same way as business names above. First by the full name of the case, usually plaintiff versus defendant, and then by the surname of the defendant followed by the full case name, so:

Delaney vs. Richards

Richards (Delaney vs. Richards)

Index consistently using listings that help readers find information quickly and easily.

Errata

An errata section is used to alert the reader to any errors that were discovered during production that are uncorrected in the narrative. For publishers who run thousands of books in a single press run, these sections are necessary because they will not issue a corrected edition until the print run is sold out. Fortunately, if you use one of the print-on-demand printers that does not charge to upload a new version, you can correct errors as you find them by uploading a new interior file. There would be no need for an errata section.

An errata section is organized in order of the errors with the chapter number and page number, followed by what is listed and the correction. For example:

Chapter 2, page 26: 21 May 1767 should read 21 May 1867

Chapter 2, page 33: Richard S. Burton should read Richard L. Burton

Colophon

A colophon is the design and production credits for the book: who created the cover and interior, the fonts and paper used, and the name of the printer. This information can also go on the copyright page above the copyright notice and cataloging data.

Excerpt

If you have written other books, or are writing or planning to write additional books, include an excerpt from another book at the end of this one, especially in an electronic version. In an electronic version you can also include a live link to your website, a blog where you will update readers on the progress of a new book, or to a place where the other book(s) is sold. Include the full links in your print edition as well so interested readers can find you online.

Include something exciting or useful in the excerpt. Then, tell the reader why they may be interested in other books you have written. Ask readers to check out the link. This is referred to as a "call to action" in marketing. You could also include a line such as, "If you enjoyed this book and would like to purchase a copy for a family member."

Format the excerpt the same way as the body text. If you have many other books, list them at the end of the excerpt so that interested readers can browse your list of titles. Include links for each of these titles as well.

Order Form

Including an order form is one way to make sure an interested person who has found your book in a library has a way to contact you to buy their own copy. Not everyone uses the Internet to place orders, even today.

An order form should occur on the last page, and should include:

- Your name or your company name
- Your address (where they should send the order)
- Your website address
- A call to action ("If you enjoyed this book and would like to buy a copy for a family member ...")
- All titles available (cross-sell your other books)
- The price of each item
- Shipping and handling charges for each item
- A discount for ordering more than one book (free shipping perhaps)
- Any additional merchandise you have to offer (photographic reprints or family tree charts, for example)
- A place to total the order
- A place to fill out their name, address, email address (make this area big enough for the person ordering to write legibly)
- An explanation of the payment methods you will accept (check, money order, PayPal or credit card)

Creating order forms can be tricky. Find a good catalog order form and use it as your guide.

In the back matter, you have an opportunity to include whatever did not fit easily into the body of the book, or to clarify terms used or mistakes discovered after the typesetting was finished.

The most important item in the back matter is the index. Every non-fiction book must have one, including a family history. Even if you forgo the place names and subject entries, an every-name index has become the genealogical standard. The index is also a good marketing tool. Most people are delighted to see their names in the index and want to read more.

As the publisher, everything else in the back matter is up to you.

It may seem as if there are a lot of rules to follow for typesetting, but it is the attention to detail in the typesetting that will make your book look like it has been professionally published.

Chapter 8

Images for Print

Pick your images as carefully as you pick your words. Use images to help readers *see* the story you are telling. Use charts to show relationships and to help keep names straight. Use photographs of ancestors if you have them. Use illustrations or maps to demonstrate concepts, give directions, or show routes and distances. Gather any visual clues the reader may need to fully understand the story.

Since you may own many of the images you want to use, the section on scanning (below) has instructions for preparing images for print production.

One word about organizing images—at some point, you will need to have every image digitized and ready to place in the layout. Rather than creating a huge backlog of items to scan or photograph, do your best to digitize as you find the item, then create folders on the computer by chapter, person or subject. You may find that you have so many images of one family, that creating sub-folders by decade would help. Share with others as you scan. That may encourage cousins to scan and share with you, too.

Charts

Use charts to show relationships. Generation charts or pedigree charts are good visual references for readers who are not as familiar with different branches of the family as you are. Generation charts show three or more generations at a glance. Most genealogy software will produce a generation chart at the push of a button. If you want to fancy up the chart, you can add photographs or background pictures. You could also use third party software designed to make elegant, detailed generation charts.

For your book, however, keep the charts as simple as possible so that they are easy to read on a single book page. It is difficult to include more than four to five generations on an 8.5" x 11" page even without the birth, death and marriage dates or locations. You do not need to include full information if it will not fit, simply birth and death dates, for example.

If you have a fancier chart with pictures or illustrations, offer it as a separate product (printed sheet or PDF) to people who are interested in the book.

Another useful visual reference is a family group sheet showing a nuclear family—a couple and their children in the order in which the children were born. Genealogy software creates these as well. The charts can be modified to show multiple marriages with all of the children (full and half-siblings), as well as the children's spouses.

Photographs

Include personal photographs of as many of the central characters as you can. Conduct an images review of what you already have for each person or family. Then, reach out to your extended family to find photographs you still need.

Ask other researchers. Look in local archives, newspapers or historical society collections. Search military history websites or museums. Try eBay. You never know where you may find a photograph.

Depending upon the story, you may want more than portrait photographs of the people— animals and pets, for example, if animals were important to the family. Unfortunately, most people do not take pictures of the scenes they see every day such as the rooms in their own homes, their offices, or of their cars— even today, when photography is so cheap. If your story occurs more than 50 years ago, you may find nothing but portrait photographs, and even those may be relatively few.

If the story takes place in the recent past, look for pictures of your ancestors' homes, businesses or neighborhoods. If not, search for historic photographs. Even if you do not use all of these photographs in the book, they may be helpful to you when describing scenes to your reader.

Historic Photographs

You may want to expand the photographs beyond your own family collection to include historical photographs of the region or era.

Searching the Internet. While it is easy to locate images by using the images feature on a search engine, the Internet is not the best place to find digital files of images that will look good in print. For print production, you need an image at 300 ppi at the size you want to display it. You will need a higher resolution image than most of what you will find on the Internet because websites use images that have been down-sampled to 72 ppi for quick retrieval and display.

Having said that, you *can* use the search engines to locate collections that contain the images you want. There are collections where images are free from copyright restrictions, and others where you may have to pay a fee in order to include a photograph in your book.

Locating Photograph Collections. Use the "Images" feature on Google or Bing to search for a location or an event. For example, I searched for the "Battle of Vera Cruz, Mexican War" and came up with dozens of digital images of paintings of that battle including one that came from the War Memorial page at Columbia University's website (warmemorial.columbia.edu). Clicking on the link to the original image took me to the Roll of Honor for the Mexican War. From there I was able to obtain the address for the Office of the Provost at Columbia University to contact them for permission to use the image, as well as to obtain a better, higher-resolution version to use in my book.

Bing has an interesting feature on its Images page called "Image Match." By clicking on an image, then using the Image Match feature, the search engine will list other places online where that image is found. In this case, I found the same image on the Library of Congress website in several varieties including a digitized version from color film, another from a color slide, and a black-and-white version, all with links to images with resolutions high enough to use in a book. The information about the image indicated that there are no known restrictions on publication. Good news, indeed.

Sources of Royalty Free Images. The following are websites where you may find photographs or illustrations free from copyright restrictions meaning you can include them in our book without permission or fees. Proper attribution, however, is a must.

Library of Congress Photographs (www.loc.gov/pictures/). Each image within the pictures collection at the Library of Congress has an indicator of whether the image has any known rights restrictions. The images in the American Memory Project within the Library of Congress are gathered from other collections, so check with the owner for permissions to use those photographs.

Flickr: The Commons (www.flickr.com/commons) is an area where contributors who own the photographs have contributed them without rights restrictions. Flickr is also the host of many museum and archive photographic collections, although, unless you find the image among the commons, ask permission to use it.

Getty Images Stock Photos (www.gettyimages.com/creativeimages/royalty-free). While Getty mostly sells images, it has made a collection available without copyright restrictions. Please do not be tempted to use one of their images that *is* rights restricted, however, without paying for use. Getty is known for its hardball tactics to extract compensation if you use an image without permission.

Ancestry.com has a postcard collection consisting of thousands of images from around the world. Old postcards are a great source of location, builting and event images.

Wikimedia Commons (commons.wikimedia.org) has millions of images without licensing restrictions contributed by the individuals who own them.

Again, proper attribution is a must.

Sources of Rights-Managed Images. Rights-managed images are those that you may license for use. The following sell low-cost, rights-managed images:

- Shutterstock (www.shutterstock.com)
- Dreamstime (www.dreamstime.com)
- MorgueFile (www.morguefile.com)

Historical Societies. Many local historical societies have photographic prints, slides or negatives in their collections that have not been digitized or cataloged online. The same is true of some local libraries. It pays to call and ask. Explain that you want the image for a family history. The fees can be negotiated if the institution will not make the images available to you without cost.

Ideas for Images. The following sites have millions of images of everything imaginable. If you are cannot put your finger on just the right image to help tell the story, you may find it at one of these websites.

ClickAmericana (www.clickamericana.com) has images covering every decade from the 1820s to the 1980s. ClickAmericana has such a good collection of images that you are certain to get a few ideas, and the site encourages sharing to Facebook, Twitter or Pinterest.

Retronaut (www.retronaut.com) describes itself as a photographic time machine. Retronaut has partnered with museums and archives around the world to create this digital collection.

Mountain West Digital Library (www.mwdl.org) is a portal to the image resources of several historical societies and universities in the western states.

Panoramio (www.panoramio.com) is a user-generated Wiki site where photographers post their own images. Panoramio is a good resource for modern photographs of the places your ancestors once lived. Ask for permission. Often, the photographer is flattered that you want to use the image and only asks for proper photo credit.

You may find many uses for modern photographs. The sites above are also sources for images of what places look like today, for people in period clothing, objects found in museums, or full-color images of historic places. In fact, you may find much better images taken with modern equipment than historic photographs.

Digitally Altering Photographs

Most photographs could use a little touching up, either to lighten areas that are a little too dark, to sharpen edges, or increase the contrast. Most image editing programs such as Photoshop or Photoshop Elements allow you to make these corrections easily.

The corrections that are not quite as easy are those that help re-build parts of a damaged photograph or those that eliminate unwanted or distracting elements. (For more information refer to the section Enhance, Repair and Retouch below.)

Color or Black-and-White?

Not all photographs look their best when re-printed in a book. You can test how each photograph will look by creating a digital scrapbook, of sorts, with all of the images you are considering. Use Lulu to print a private book as a proof. That way, you will see each image as it will look printed in black-and-white so that you can reject some images or fix others that look washed out or too dark.

Taking New Photographs

There is no time like the present to take a few new photographs. Even if you do not use them in this book project, ask for updated photographs of the people in your extended family every so often. Asking for recent photographs can help open doors to other areas where you want help from family members or other researchers, such as information or old photos.

Heirlooms

Objects are difficult to scan, so they should be photographed. If there are heirlooms spread throughout your family that you want to show in the book, ask family members to photograph them for you (if you are not in the area to do so).

Small objects, such as china or jewelry, often look best when isolated in a studio box with a neutral background and even lighting. Larger objects may have to be photographed in place.

Good lighting is key to good photographs. In most cases, opening curtains for natural light or placing reading lamps to shine on the object will be enough light to take a good indoor photograph with proper camera settings.

Artwork

Artwork, like other objects, is difficult to scan—easier to photograph. The key to photographing artwork is to make sure the camera is lined up in a way that keeps the image square, so that you do not create distortions—either narrower at the top than at the bottom, or narrower on one side than the other. These distortions can be fixed in your image editing program, but you will save yourself time if you take a good photograph to begin with.

Research the artwork or heirlooms you discover. Readers may be interested to know, for example, that a desk that has been in your family for 150 years was hand-crafted in New England and brought by train to Wisconsin. Or, that your aunt has a set of dinnerware popular in the 1920s and sold in dime stores.

Tombstones

Tombstone photographs are common in family histories. Even though Internet sharing sites such as Findagrave (www.findagrave.com) have made it easy to obtain tombstone photographs thanks to willing volunteers, I have mixed feelings about using tombstone photographs in book where there is limited real estate on the page. Personally, I would rather show these photographs on my online tree rather than use them in a family history—unless the tombstone is beautifully carved, in a unique location or particularly interesting. If a tombstone photograph is the only remembrance you have, then by all means, use it.

Location Photographs

While it is important to find good historic photographs or paintings that show the area as it looked while your ancestor was alive, there are some instances in which a photograph of what the place looks like today would be appropriate as well. If you have both a modern and a historic photograph, create a side-by-side composite for comparison.

While You Are on a Research Trip

If you are taking a research trip, schedule plenty of time to take an abundance of photographs. Digital photography is cheap, so shoot away. You may not use all of them in this book project, but they will be available to you or other family members for future projects.

Bracket your shots. Most digital cameras will allow you to alter the speed or the aperture from shot to shot. Some do so in a three-shot burst for you, although you must hold still until the camera completes the three shots. By bracketing, the camera will use different settings to alter the amount of light in the photograph. By bracketing, you are likely to take at least one usable shot from the three-shot group without having to alter it in your photo editing program.

Take establishing shots. The best example I can give of this is to take a picture of the sign at the cemetery entrance, and then a few shots of the view within the cemetery to give readers an idea of what the landscape is like. In a town, take a few photographs of the landscape as you come into the town, and a few of the town square.

Take encapsulating shots. At a grave site, take a photograph of the entire stone. In the town square, take a shot of the whole courthouse.

Take closeups. Make sure you can read names and dates when you get home with the photographs, so take closeups. Taking closeups will also remind you to look carefully at the entire tombstone from all sides, so you do not miss anything. In town, take photographs of the historic markers close enough that you can read them when you return home.

Take both vertical and horizontal shots. You will not know how a photograph may fit best into the book's layout until much later.

Take as many shots during your research trip as you think you will need for this project and other future projects. It is frustrating to get home and discover you have missed something important.

Panoramas

Panoramic photographs sometimes tell the story better than a single photograph can, and they are easy to create. If you want readers to experience how wide open the family homestead was, how close together the homes were on your family's street, or where buildings were in relation to other buildings, panoramic photographs are the way to go.

There are many image-editing programs, such as Photoshop (or Photoshop Elements) that will stitch together different shots to create a single image. It can be tricky to stitch together two historic photographs if the horizon lines or focal distances are different. Editing prior to stitching can help.

If you are taking new photographs to create a panorama, overlap the shots by about thirty percent. Do not change the focal distance while you are shooting the series, and try to keep the horizon line at the same position in the viewfinder as you shoot. If you are not a steady hand, a tripod can help with this.

For panorama purposes, I shoot a scene first going from left to right, and then repeat the series going the other direction. Sometimes, shots taken going one direction come out better than the other.

Most of us take photographs according to long-established personal habits. We shoot from the same standing position, from the same distance, from the same angle, or all horizontal. Your book may be more interesting, however, with a few out-of-the-ordinary photographs.

Documents and Memorabilia

Most family histories include at least a few documents so that readers can see for themselves the proof you have for your stories. Think about how you are using the real estate on the page, and whether what you are showing is so important that the reader will want to see it. Census records, for example, can be boring unless they show something extraordinary. You can add the information contained in the record as a part of the storytelling without having to show the actual census for each decade. If your ancestor showed up in the census at Buckingham Palace, however, that would be another matter.

The following are examples of documents your reader may be interested in: an ornate marriage certificate (the modern versions are not much to look at); a passenger list showing the name of the ship, its captain and your family; a land patent showing a map of the property; or a document with an ancestor's signature on it. Signatures are fabulous because they are so personal.

Some items are considered ephemera or memorabilia rather than documents, but are welcome in a family history, such as a letterhead from your ancestor's business; a newspaper clipping; a funeral card; a playbill if your ancestor was in a show; a school report card, and so on.

The documents most handy for establishing relationships within families and laying down the facts for the storytelling are not always the ones that readers will want to see, even if they are mighty interesting to the person doing the research. What *should* make the cut for the book are those documents that help tell the story *and* are visually interesting. In fact, photographs or illustrations may be better than documents for that purpose.

Illustrations

There are times when an illustration is better than a photograph. Before photography, paintings were used to illustrate an event or to capture the likeness of a person. At ruins, for example, you are likely to find an artist's rendering of what a place probably looked like, since there may be no paintings or drawings from the era to show the place as it once looked.

There are times when a line drawing is better than a photograph to to illustrate an event. Think about how you use maps online today. If you want to see what a place looks like, you may prefer the street view (a photograph), but if you need to drive there, a standard street map (an illustration) would be easier to follow.

There are rich sources of illustrations online. The key, again, is finding files with sufficient resolution to look good in print.

You may find an image that is out of copyright, such as a line drawing or lithograph from a 19th Century magazine. The trick is locating an original and producing a good scan or photograph. There are stock photography companies that also offer line illustrations free, but in most cases, you must pay to use the image.

If you are looking for house plans, Architectural Designs (www.architecturaldesigns.com), has plans with photographs and floor plan illustrations as PDFs for download. These plans are for houses to build today, but are based upon historical designs. The floor plans in the PDFs may not be of sufficient quality for re-print, but you could re-create one as a simple pen and ink drawing to use in its stead.

Another option is to find an illustrator who is able to create original drawings. (See Working with an Illustrator.)

Maps

Create a list of places for which a map may help readers get their bearings.

As a part of your research, locating a map created at the time your ancestor lived is an invaluable source of accurate information. Such a map enables you and your readers to see what streets existed, or how far the town extended, for example.

Historic Maps

Fortunately, there are many places that have good map collections. Check with the major universities (e.g. Harvard and Yale), large libraries (e.g. Newberry Library and the Free Library of Philadelphia) and the local college or university in the area you are researching.

The following is a list of good map collections online:

- Library of Congress Maps Collection (www.loc.gov/maps/).
- David Rumsey Map Collection (www.davidrumsey.com).
- Perry-Castaneda Library Map Collection at the University of Texas (www.lib.utexas.edu/maps/).
- American Geographical Society Digital Map Collection (collections.lib.uwm.edu/cdm/landingpage/collection/agdm).

Modern Maps

There are instances when a modern map may help put the story into context. A modern map can show how places are related, how many different locations an ancestor lived, or how far they traveled. Modern maps can be useful for this type of demonstration.

There are searchable modern maps at: MapQuest (www.mapquest.com), Bing (www.bing.com), and Google (www.google.com).

Each has fairly generous Terms of Use that allow you to capture a screenshot of a map and re-produce it elsewhere as long as you are not using the map, itself, for commercial gain. Check the terms on the site before you spend too much time gathering maps as screenshots.

Google, Bing and MapQuest each offer street maps, topographical features and satellite views. All three offer directions and information about local services such as restaurants, hotels and local attractions.

Google and Bing offer GPS coordinates and closeup views—Google calls it Street View, Bing calls it Bird's Eye and Streetside. These features are helpful in determining what exists at a location currently. Not all areas are updated frequently by Bing or Google frequently, so looking at the date watermarked on the map will give you an idea of how long ago the view was captured.

Google allows you to sign in to your Google account and create maps with your own map points, to save or share by email. They also offer developer tools to create your own maps and place them on your website or blog. The Community Walk feature allows you to create a map with personalized points, and add photos, videos and comments.

Google Maps will give you the outline of an entire county by searching for the county and state. Since so much genealogical research is conducted county by county, showing an outline of a county with the cities and roads visible may be helpful.

Bing Maps has a feature that is helpful when filling in missing location data in your research. Bing Maps will give you the county name if you have a city and a state, but do not know the county. The Country > State > County > City information will appear at the top of the map to the right of the centering tool. If you put in Nederland, Colorado, for example, you will see: United States, CO, Boulder Co, Nederland.

Screen Captures

Screen captures are not an issue if you are planning to publish in an electronic form. They can be an issue, however, if you want them to look good in print.

Your computer, whether a PC or a Mac, probably has a screen capture feature. On the PC, press Control + Alt + PrtScrn, then paste the image into another program such as Word or Photoshop. Unfortunately, standard screen capture software does not always create an image that looks good in print because the software is only able to capture what is on the screen displayed at 72 to 96 ppi.

SnagIt (www.techsmith.com/snagit.html) has been the industry leader in screen capture for years. It has the most options for gathering screen captures from different sources such as websites or video, and the ability to edit and enhance captured images. The cost is around $50, but if screen captures are important to your printed book, it may be worth the purchase.

To obtain the best possible screen capture, increase the size of an image displayed on screen by zooming in (Control+Shift+[+] on a PC), which makes the image bigger on the screen when you capture it. Ideally, you will end up with a screen capture at a size large enough to create a 300 ppi image at the size you want for the book. For example, if you were to capture an image on screen at 16" x 12" at 72 ppi, that would translate into a pixel size of 1152 x 864. The largest 300 ppi image you could create from that pixel size would be 3.84" (1152 divided by 300) x 2.88" (864 divided by 300).

Family histories satisfy the curiosity. Not only will your family members be curious about the stories you have to tell, but also about what their ancestors looked like, and what their homes, land or businesses may have looked like. A simple pedigree chart can answer questions quicker than an entire chapter sometimes. A beautifully printed marriage license or certificate of achievement will delight your readers.

Use as many images as you think you need to tell the story. Leave out images if they are included solely to document facts. Seek out instead, memorabilia or ephemera that helps define the era, or maps that put the stories into context. If the book grows too big because it is beautifully illustrated, you can always split it into more than one volume.

Help from Family

Ask family members to drag out their boxes of photos or photo albums to help you locate the images you need.

Use social media to reach out. It is amazing how many cousins you can rustle up on Facebook, Twitter, or LinkedIn.

Although you can post photos to most social media sites, there are dedicated photo sharing sites such as:

- Flickr (www.flickr.com)
- Shutterfly (www.shutterfly.com)
- DotPhoto (www.dotphoto.com)

Some photo sharing sites will let your family members download the digital images or order prints for themselves. Encourage family members to use the photographs you have shared. Holidays or family reunions are a good time to make use of the images. Besides, you may find your images coming back to you through talented or creative cousins in the form of scrapbooks, photo books or other photo-inspired gifts.

Help from Strangers

Sometimes, we need help from complete strangers. Use the message boards on the major genealogy sites where other researchers may be working on the same family lines and may have images.

Look for blogs with photographs of the area your ancestors lived. Bloggers familiar with an area can be a great resource for research help or may have suggestions for images.

There are helpful photographers on Findagrave, Flickr or Panoramio. Oftentimes, a photo credit is enough for the photographer to grant permission to use the image.

If you cannot find exactly the right photograph, sometimes you need only ask to have an image taken for you. If you want a photograph of a school your ancestor attended, for example, you may find a helpful stranger associated with one of the websites above, willing to make a trip over to the school to take the picture. The staff at the local library or historical society may also know of a volunteer willing to help you.

For the best results, be specific about what you want. Explain that the photograph will be used in a print book so you need a high-resolution image. If you need a photograph of a building with enough clear blue sky above it to accommodate your title and subtitle, say so. Ask for both horizontal and vertical images if you do not know yet what you need for the layout. You are more likely to receive exactly what you need if you are specific.

After obtaining what you need, a nice thank you goes a long way. (This applies to family members as well.) Send a hand-written note, or a small gift card for someone who has gone the extra mile for you. Consider also emailing a PDF of the chapter showing the photograph(s) and proper credit to the photographer.

Chapter 9

Scanning Basics for Print

From the scanner's point of view, there are only three types of items it can scan—reflective items (photographs or documents), negative transparencies (film negatives), or positive transparencies (slides). Because the scanner will treat each of these types differently, you may need different software settings or different equipment to obtain the best scan.

You will save a lot of time and effort making your images ready for your book if you produce a good scan from the start.

Your goal while scanning is to create an image large enough to look good in print, at the size you want to display the image. Once you have the largest scan you will need, you can scale, downsample or size the image for other uses such as a website, an electronic book, or to share on social media.

Scanners

There are many different types of scanners including: dedicated flatbed, all-in-one, photo, film, slide hand-held, and microfilm/microfiche. Each has advantages and disadvantages.

Dedicated Flatbed Scanners

For most book projects, a dedicated flatbed scanner is what you need. The major scanner manufacturers such as HP, Epson, Canon or Xerox (among others) include their own software, most of which will work for your book project. Some dedicated flatbed scanners are designed to scan photographs rather than documents, so the software may include Digital ICE (digital image correction and enhancement). Most photo-priority flatbed scanners allow you to make corrections to the image as it is scanned.

Not all dedicated flatbed scanners are equipped to scan transparencies, either film negatives or slides. Transparencies require a dual light source and an adapter to hold the film or negative during scanning, allowing the light source to shine through the transparency. Because of the small size of the transparency (usually one inch square or less), the software must be able to scan at much higher resolution to obtain a print-ready digital image. (More about resolution, shortly.)

Film or Slide Scanners

Dedicated film or slide scanners have no glass between the light source and the transparency to prevent distortion. These scanners also use a cool light source to keep from warping the film or slide, and the software included will be capable of high resolutions. Some of these scanners have a feeder for 35mm film strips or a stacking tray for slides. If you have older, large negatives, you will need a flatbed scanner with adapter trays to hold those negative sizes.

Hand-Held Scanners

Hand-held scanners (or wand scanners) are convenient, but often it is difficult to produce a good scan if your hands are not steady or the object is not perfectly flat.

One hand-held scanner I like, however, is the FlipPal (flip-pal.com). This mini-scanner was designed with the genealogist in mind. It is small, lightweight, and is approved for use in repositories such as the National Archives. Even though the surface area of the FlipPal cannot scan a full piece of paper at once, the software that comes with the FlipPal has a stitching function to put documents back together after they have been scanned in pieces. The one disadvantage to the FlipPal is how little control you have over making corrections as the scan is being made. It is a trade off—the ease and convenience of being able to scan photographs or documents at a relative's house, versus producing the best scan possible. Better to obtain the image while you can and make corrections in your image editing software later.

Microfilm/Microfiche Scanners

You may run into a microfilm or a microfiche scanner while conducting research. Many Family History Centers and libraries across the country have them. It may be more convenient to save your scanned images as PDFs while you are researching because they are easy to read on your computer later using the free Adobe Acrobat Reader software. If you *know*, however, that you want to use an image of a document in your book, obtain a higher resolution JPG while you are at the library. Take both. Look for the settings in the scanning software to change back and forth from JPG to PDF.

Most word processors and page layout programs will not treat a PDF the same way they will a JPG. Most will not allow you to place a PDF directly into a document. Use an image editing program to convert the PDF to a JPG, PNG or TIFF.

All-in-One Scanners

For those of you who own 3-in-1 or 4-in-1 scanners (scan, copy, print, fax), the scanning software that came with the machine may be fairly rudimentary. Dedicated flatbed scanners tend to come with better software including SilverFast (www.silverfast.com) or VueScan (www.hamrick.com). This software can be purchased as stand-alone products. You may find that once you have better software, an all-in-one will do what you need it to, as long as you do not have transparencies. In my research to date, I have not found a 3-in-1 or 4-in-1 scanner that included a transparency adapter.

Resolution

First, let us be clear about some terminology. You may see the acronyms dpi and lpi and ppi used interchangeably. They are not exactly the same, however. Dots per inch (dpi) is an old printer's term that refers to the number of horizontal dots per inch in a halftone. If you look closely at a photographic image in a pre-digital-era newspaper, you will see the dots used to make up the photograph. This was a clever way to simulate the effect of a solid image on a page. The same technology was used for most commercial printing that produced magazines, maps, booklets or brochures.

Lines per inch (lpi) is another way to measure the number of dots per inch in a halftone, although this is a vertical measurement. The more lines per inch, the sharper the image. Magazines have more lines per inch than newspapers.

Pixels per inch (ppi) is the proper way to describe resolution in the digital era. If you zoom in to a digital photograph closely enough, you will be able to see each pixel. Pixels are square, whereas dots are round. The higher the number of pixels per inch, the higher the resolution in the image, and the better it will look when printed.

What resolution you need depends upon the physical size of the image you want to display, and how you will display it.

Scan high and use low, meaning that you want a scan that is as big physically—in inches—as you will display in print. Most books are (physically) 8.5" x 11" or smaller. If you subtract room for margins, about the biggest image you will need is 8" x 10". If you go wild with the print size for a coffee table book, you may need a larger image.

For print, the resolution must be at least 300 ppi for photographs. Line art (think handwriting in a document) may look better at 600 ppi because the edges of the lines will be crisper.

Many of the older photographs you will encounter may be physically small. It was not until the 1990s that photography became so much cheaper. Today, you can buy a poster-sized print for less than what a school portrait cost in the 1940s.

Take a 1" x 1.5" slide or school portrait as our example. In order to create a proportionally-equivalent 8" x 12" digital image at 300 ppi, the final file size must be 2400 x 3600 pixels (8" x 300 ppi and 12" x 300 ppi). If you are scanning a 1" x 1.5" slide, in order to end up with a file at 2400 x 3600 pixels, you will need to scan at 2400 ppi (1" x 2400 ppi = 2400 pixels wide and 1.5" x 2400 ppi = 3600 pixels long).

A common pre-1950s photograph size was (in inches) 3 x 4.5, so let us use that as an example. If we want to use a photograph that size in print at (in inches) 6 x 9, then we will need a final file size of 1800 pixels x 2700 pixels. In order to achieve that resolution, you must scan at 600 ppi (3" x 600 ppi = 1800 pixels wide and 4.5" x 600 ppi = 2700 pixels long).

If you are planning to acquire images from either a stock photography company, or a library or archive, ask for the image resolution needed to print at 300 ppi in the physical size you want for the page or the cover.

There may be other uses for your photographs at much lower resolution, such as an eBook, to email to cousins, to post on social media sites or your online tree. As long as you start with an image large enough to look good in print, scaling down is easy with good results. Scaling up is not. An image that has been scaled up may look fine on the screen because your computer screen can only display an image at 72-96 ppi. A scaled-up photograph may look fine in your word processing program, but pixelated or blurry when printed in a book.

There is also a difference between scaling a photograph and stretching it. Your word processing program will allow you to take an image, insert it into the text, then adjust the display size by pulling the corners. This is not scaling the photograph, this is stretching it. Stretching causes even worse results in print than scaling an image up to a larger size.

Scaling a photograph means opening it into an image editing program and changing the physical size of the image. You will achieve far more consistent results on the press, if you scan the image to the correct size first, and then place the image into the layout in the correct size and resolution.

File Size

Do not over-scan your images. To keep the file size of the final book manageable, create images at a size that will look good in print, but not any bigger. In other words, scan your image so that you could print an 16" x 24" photograph to give to a cousin (the biggest use you may have for the image), but adjust it down proportionally before placing it into your book layout.

To adjust the image down proportionally, determine the final size you want the image to be on the page, for example (in inches) 3 x 3.75, and use your image editing program to make the physical size of the image smaller.

What you do not want to do, is place the largest size image into your manuscript, and squeeze it into its final size by dragging the corners. This will make the physical size smaller, but does not alter the file size. If your original image is 8" x 10" at 300 ppi, it would have a physical size of 2400 pixels x 3000 pixels. If you squish those pixels closer together to make them fit into a 3" x 3.75" space, your resolution will go up from 300 ppi to 800 ppi (2400 pixels divided by 3" = 800 ppi and 3000 pixels divided by 3.75" is 800 ppi).

Print publication requires a final image resolution at 300 ppi. Use your image editing program to reduce the physical size of the photograph to 3" x 3.75" which is a proportional reduction, while maintaining the resolution of 300 ppi, giving you a final image size of 900 pixels (3" x 300 ppi) x 1125 pixels (3.75" x 300 ppi).

Color Depth

Color depth affects file size. The greater the color depth, the more color possibilities there are and the larger the file size. A black-and-white image (e.g. a printed document) has only 1 bit of color depth because there is only one color—black. The other color, white, is the paper color. A black-and-white photograph is actually made up of shades of black, so an 8-bit file would contain 256 shades of gray. A 24-bit file could contain up to 16.7 million colors and so on up to 36-bit and 48-bit files.

Scanning a photograph to display on the side of a bus, would need as much color information as possible since the image is so large, and too little color information can cause banding rather than smooth transitions between shades.

Many of the newer scanners offer greater than 24-bit depth. The biggest difference between 24-bit and 48-bit scans is in the file size. Reserve the 48-bit setting for scanning negatives and slides. Anything you want to scan for a printed book (and even less so for an eBook or digital file) can be scanned at 24-bit color depth and look great. There is no need to over-scan color depth.

Color Density

To achieve the blackest blacks and the whitest whites, in other words, the greatest possible dynamic range for color in your images, you may want a scanner that captures the greatest image density, not necessarily the greatest bit depth. Be forewarned, however, the higher the image density, the higher the cost of the scanner, and realistically, unless you are planning a high-end, glossy photo book, the end results on the page will not be any better.

Color Space

Color space matters to some printers for some print jobs. Chances are good that you will not have to mess much with the color space during your book project, but, just in case, here is a quick explanation of what color space means.

RGB

The RBG color space (red, green, blue) is used on computer monitors and other digital screens. RGB is also fine for printing photographs. RGB is preferred for images in eBooks that will be displayed on digital screens. The most common file format for RGB images is JPG. When you are scanning photographs, it is acceptable to scan them as RGB images and save them as JPGs.

CMYK

The CMYK color space (cyan, magenta, yellow, black) is necessary to use an off-set press and print in full color. Cyan, magenta, yellow and black are the four process colors that are combined to create full-color images. For most books, you do not need to worry about the CMYK color space. It is acceptable to leave your images in their original RGB color space when creating your final file. Let the printer convert the images to CMYK based upon the equipment they have to generate the best results.

Grayscale

Become familiar with the grayscale color space. For books with black-and-white images in the interior (forget the covers for right now, almost all covers will be created in full-color), convert your images to grayscale before you place them into the layout. Another reason to do this, is to see how the image will look when printed in black-and-white. Not all color images make good black-and-whites. If there are not enough shades of gray, the finer details will be lost.

Convert black-and-white originals to grayscale. It is possible to scan directly into grayscale, and some scanners have good grayscale settings, but most of the time you will achieve better results if you scan black-and-white photographs in full color, then use your image editing program to convert the image to grayscale.

Bitmap

The bitmap color space is one that you may use, but infrequently. On occasion, you will find that a document or line drawing is easier to read if scanned as a bitmap. The bitmap color space only contains black and white, there are no shades of gray. The scanner will force each pixel in the image to be one color or the other. Sometimes, especially if there is a noisy background on a document, the type or handwriting is clearer when scanned as a bitmap image.

File Formats

Digital image file formats are either compressed, or non-compressed. A non-compressed format will retain the most information and will create larger file sizes than a compressed format.

TIFF or RAW

Two non-compressed formats are TIFF (or TIF) and RAW. RAW image files can be exceedingly large because they are not compressed in any way. To compare, an image taken in my 16 MP (megapixel) camera and saved as a TIFF is about 5 MB (megabytes) in size, whereas the same image saved in RAW format runs 16 MB or more. Saving images in the RAW format is an option in high-end cameras. Some scanning software will create RAW files, but unless you are planning to use your image on the cover of a high-end magazine, there is no compelling reason to create RAW files while you scan.

JPG

The most common file format for photographs is JPG (or JPEG). This is a compressed file format, and yes, you will lose information every time you open, alter and save the file, somewhat like making a photocopy of a photocopy. But, unless you alter the file hundreds of times and then blow the photo up to something large enough for the flaws to become obvious to the naked eye, do not worry about whether you scan and save your family photographs as compressed or uncompressed files. Save them as TIF or JPG, whatever is easiest to work with.

Producing a Good Scan

Before you begin scanning, clean the glass on the scanner. Unless there are smudges, compressed air or a good microcloth will do the trick. If there are smudges or fingerprints, use a good glass cleaner. Read the instructions for your scanner to make sure an alcohol-based glass cleaner is safe. Then spray the cloth, not the scanner glass and clean the glass often. Small specks of dust will show up in the scans (magnified if you are scanning film or slides) and it takes much more time to fix the dust particle flaws in your image editing program, than it does to eliminate them from the scanner.

Do not damage originals in order to scan them. Do not cut them or try to make repairs, and please *do not* clean the photograph unless you *really* know what you are doing. Any effort to alter the surface of a photograph can damage or destroy it. If you are in doubt, seek the help of a photo restoration company. If you have delicate photographs, it is always safer to re-photograph, than to put them on the scanner exposed to a strong light source.

Photographing a Photograph

The trick to photographing a photograph is to use a macro setting on your digital camera that allows the lens to be close to the photograph while keeping it in focus. Fll the frame with the photograph to take as large an image as possible.

Keep the angles consistent so the photograph is not distorted in the digital image. This means placing the photograph on a level surface (wall or table) and setting the camera up to shoot straight on. If the camera is angled in any way, the original photograph will not look square in the new image. You can fix distortions later in your image editing program, but you will save a great deal of time, if you take a good photograph to begin with.

If your old photograph has curled or has warped, introduce a little humidity before unrolling it. I have had good luck with my own photographs by steaming up the bathroom and taking the photograph into the bathroom away from the faucet where the hot water is running. I have only tried this on modern photographs (less than 50 years old). I would not attempt this on any photograph that was made before modern fixatives were used. If you are at all in doubt, take the photograph to a photo restoration company for help before you begin. Never try to force a photograph to unroll. Once the emulsion on a photograph cracks, you cannot undo the damage.

For photographs that uncurl easily, placing a piece of non-glare glass over the top may help to hold it down while you photograph. Even non-glare glass can yield reflections, though, so watch for flares from light sources such as lamps, overhead lighting or windows.

If you are not a steady hand, use a tripod. In fact, a tripod with a scientific arm that allows the camera to point straight down, is the easiest way to obtain great digital images of photographs or documents.

Scanning Slides or Film Negatives

Before you scan slides or film negatives, use compressed air to clean them. If you remove a slide or negative from a plastic film sleeve or run a micro-cloth over it, static electricity can attract even more dust. Be careful not to use the spray air too close to the slide or negative because of the moisture that comes from the spray.

Scanner Software

Get to know your scanner and the software it came with. Locate the feature that allows you to change the physical file size and resolution while scanning. It will not take you long to be able to calculate what you will need to achieve a 300 ppi resolution for images at the maximum size you will display them in your book. Remember to scan high, use low. It is better to create an image that is bigger than what you will ever need and scale it down to fit the page, than to scan an image too small and scale it up to size.

Some scanning software features will correct image flaws while scanning. Some software has very good automatic settings for color, contrast, brightness, sharpness, and saturation or neutralization. Others do not. Experiment with a few flawed images to find out what your software is capable of correcting well.

Save Time Scanning

Most scanning software allows you to preview the image before you scan it. In the beginning, this feature will save you a lot of time having to look back and forth between the scanning software and your image editing program to make sure you got the image you wanted in the scan. After a time, especially if you are scanning the same types of items that are also the same size, you may be able to skip the preview to save time. The trick is to keep similar items together, the black-and-white photographs for example, or the images with similarly fading tints.

While it is tempting to place as many photographs on the plate as possible and scan them all at once as one big photograph, avoid this. Not only will you spend more time turning them into separate photographs later in your image editing program, but the scanner will take readings across a bunch of different photographs which will give the automatic correction settings a difficult time determining what should be corrected. The results are often bad scans.

Some scanning software allows you to batch scan everything on the plate with separate settings for each item. This feature *will* save time because each object on the plate is being analyzed and scanned individually.

The straighten and flip settings can save time. Even if you place a photograph on the plate perfectly, closing the lid may cause it to move. Allowing the scanner to straighten the photograph will save time. Same for flipping photographs—especially flipping slides and film negatives. It can be difficult to slip the slides and film strips into the holders exactly the right way each time. Look at the preview, then let the scanner turn the image right-side up or flip it on the vertical axis to make the scan match the direction of the original.

Photographs

While it would seem that scanning photographs will have fewer challenges than other types of material, it all depends upon the type of photographs you need. If you have the time, consider scanning everything you have and creating backups on external hard drives or DVDs just in case. You never know when originals will be lost or damaged.

Older photographs that have curled over the years can yield Newton Rings—distortion caused when there is distance between the photograph and the glass—when scanning. If a photograph is particularly delicate, taking a new photograph of the old photograph is always safer than putting it on the scanner and exposing it to an intense light source. If you do not have the ability to re-photograph the item, look for a studio photographer who has the right setup and lighting.

Occasionally, scanning a black-and-white photograph in full color will leave tinges of yellow, cyan or magenta in the picture. This can be fixed in your image editing program. Or, try scanning in grayscale to see if you achieve a better result.

If your book will contain only black-and-white images, it may take some experimentation not only with your scanner, but also in your image editing program to make each photograph look its best when printed in black-and-white.

It was popular for a time to print photographs on textured paper so that they looked more like a painted canvas. These photographs (mostly from the 1970s) can be a challenge to scan because the texture can cause shadows on the scan. Taking a new photograph may be the better option.

Matte prints often scan with fewer streaks or glare than glossy prints. Modern glossy prints are not so much the issue as older glossies mounted on thick paper such as those from instant cameras such as Polaroids. If you are seeing streaks in scanned images from glare off the glossy print, taking new photographs may be easier than fixing the digital images.

When a digital image is printed on uncoated paper, such as what will be used on the interior pages of your book, dot gain causes photographs to become darker than expected. You may need to lighten the shadows and mid-tones of photographs in order to make them look their best in print. This is true whether the photographs are in black-and-white or in color.

One way to create a digital image from a slide is to scan it; another is to project it onto a screen and photograph it using a digital camera. While the projector version works quite well for images that will be shown on a computer monitor, often the result in print is flat, soft or dark images that do not look as good as if you had scanned the slide directly. If a slide is particularly important to you and you cannot produce a good scan, print the slide at the size you need for the book, then scan the new photograph. This is an expensive option, however, for more than a few vital slides.

Documents and Illustrations

For the most part, documents and illustrations (line art) are easier to scan and achieve good results, than photographs. Line art such as lithographs look best when scanned at 600 to 1200 ppi to keep the edges and lines clean and crisp. Many of these images will be black-and-white, so scanning as bitmaps (BMP) which forces the image into black-and-white, may give you the best results. If the line art is in color such as a logo or sign, scan in at least 24-bit color depth to keep gradients smooth. Scanning at lower bit depths may cause banding in the colored areas.

One challenge may be the paper the item is printed on, however, since thin paper can allow printing on the reverse side to show through. If this is a problem, one option is to photocopy the originals using light settings to lessen what shows through, and then scan the lightened photocopy using settings that make the document darker.

Using Optical Character Recognition

Most scanners come with optical character recognition (OCR) software. While it may be tempting to OCR documents or passages from printed sources so that you do not have to transcribe each and every one, be careful with the results. The software works best with printed, standard font text (nothing script-like or hand-writing-like) in point sizes between six (6) (very small but still readable) and 72 (about 1 inch high) on laser or inkjet quality print or better.

Mocavo, the online genealogy search engine (www.mocavo.com), is experimenting with OCR that works on handwriting. They are the first, and they have not perfected it yet. You will not find commercially available scanner-based OCR software that can help you with handwritten documents just yet.

No matter how sophisticated your OCR software, you *must* proofread the results. It is difficult for the software to tell the difference between a "1" that looks like an "l" that looks like a "]."

The easiest OCR programs to use are those that let you correct the copy while the software is creating the text. Many of the best programs show the image in one window with the text results in another window side by side so that you can look at the original as you edit.

Maps, Newspapers and Memorabilia

If you have maps, newspaper clippings or memorabilia such as a theater program that was printed using halftones (bunches of little dots rather than a solid image like a photograph) you may have some challenges in scanning these items.

Halftones may create moire patterns (common in black-and-white images from newspapers) or rosette patterns (common in color images due to the CMYK colors used on the press). The result of scanning may be images with irregular areas, or areas that are much darker or lighter than other areas.

The ability to de-screen as you scan is a special feature in some scanning software. Software that comes with a de-screening feature will have the following settings for different types of print: art print (175 lpi), magazines (133 lpi) and newspapers (85 lpi). You will achieve the best results with the setting closest to what was used to create the original image on the press. Sometimes de-screening can soften an image too much. Sharpening can help restore the edges.

If your software does not have a de-screening feature, try scanning at a 45 degree angle. Turn the object so that it is not straight up or down (90 degrees), but at an angle (45 degrees) on the plate. Another option is to scan at twice the size you are planning to use in the book, then downsize the image so that the dots or dot patterns are not so obvious.

Objects

It is much easier to photograph objects, such as heirlooms, against a neutral background than it is to scan them. It is almost impossible to make a teacup look good sitting on a scanner. Instead of scanning dog tags, a uniform, needlework, or a picture in its frame, take a photograph.

For less than $50, you can buy a small studio lighting kit that sets up as a two-foot square box, with neutral backgrounds of several different colors, a couple of lights, and a table-top tripod. For around $200, you can buy a similar studio lighting setup to photograph larger objects such as quilts or furniture.

Art

Artwork should be photographed, not scanned, especially if the art is in a soft media such as pastels or charcoal. Pencil sketches can smudge. Oil paintings or watercolor paintings can be a challenge because of the texture of the paint or the unevenness of the canvas.

Film Negatives and Slides

The biggest issue with scanning film negatives and slides is cleaning them before you scan to minimize the dust and particle debris in the digital image and scanning at high enough resolution for your planned use.

A standard 35mm negative is not square. It measures approximately 1" x 1.5" or at a 2 x 3 ratio. If you want the digital image to fill an 8.5" x 11" page (although you will need to shrink the image to fit within your margins), you will need a digital image of 2550 pixels (8.5" x 300 pixels) by 3300 pixels (11" x 300 ppi). So the resolution for a 1" x 1.5" 35mm film negative is 2550 ppi. The ratio of standard American paper at 8.5" x 11" is not quite 2 to 3, however, so your scan at 2550 ppi will be perfect across the 8.5" top, but too long for the 11" length. Even when you adjust for the margins, cropping may be necessary. If you are thinking about printing from your digital image and want a good 12" x 18" print, scanning a 35mm negative at 4000 ppi will work.

Curled filmstrips can result in blurry scans. If absolutely necessary, the individual negatives can be cut and mounted into slide mounts, but once that is done they can no longer be printed at a standard photo lab. They will have to be processed at a specialty lab at higher cost. If you are going to cut a filmstrip, make prints first.

When scanning film negatives, scan with the emulsion (duller side) down. The emulsion side should be closest to the glass on a flatbed scanner. You can tell if you are looking at the emulsion side if the film numbers along the edge are backward.

Before you scan slides, check to see if your scanning software has adjustments for different slide types. Kodachrome slides, for example, should be scanned on a Kodachrome color setting for best results. If you have no idea what type of film was used to create your slides, you may have to play with the color adjustment settings to create the best digital image during the scan.

Tip: Although it may be tempting, once you have finished scanning, never discard the originals. Newer scanners may do a better job in the future and digital images can be lost or become corrupted.

Enhance, Repair, Retouch

Even if you achieve great scans, you may want to open each image in an image editor to take a look close up. Before you place any image into your layout, fix flaws, sharpen softly-focused images, adjust the contrast, or crop to enhance the composition. Repair damage that may have occurred from bends, breaks or mold on the surface. Restore the faded color. Fill in the dust or scratches, and correct over or underexposed areas.

There is always a bit of controversy surrounding editing or enhancing images that alters *in any way* the historical accuracy of the image, since you are using the image to tell a family history which should be historically accurate. Having said that, there is no reason not to repair or retouch photographs so that they look their best.

When does restoration become alteration? That is a matter of opinion, but I think it is fine to use a little grain reduction to make a person's skin look smooth and beautiful, or to remove red-eyes, or to whiten teeth. It is fine to crop an image to enhance the composition, or to merge two images to create a more complete picture of what a place looked like. I know I am stepping into controversial waters here, but it is acceptable to remove distracting elements from the picture even if it alters the historical accuracy of the photograph a bit. I am not advocating that you digitally cut out your ex, or blur the face of a family member you do not like. Oftentimes, however, amateur photographers take pictures without paying attention to the background, resulting in images that appear as if a telephone pole, for example, is growing from a person's head. I find it historically acceptable to remove the telephone pole.

There are many options for editing your digital images. Most computers come with simple image editing software pre-installed. There are also many websites or photo sharing sites that offer image editing tools. Some of them, such as Pixlr (pixlr.com), or Picasa (picasa.google.com), have impressive features. There are also apps by the dozen for tablets or smartphones that edit, enhance or create funky artwork from digital images. Another option is to buy a stand-alone image editor such as Corel PaintShop Pro or Photoshop (the full version is pricey, but Photoshop Elements, the consumer edition, is not).

Before you alter any digital image, make a copy and keep the original scan in a safe place. Work off the copy in case you make an alteration that you regret.

This book is not the place for a complete primer on digital image restoration. Consult, *Digital Restoration from Start to Finish* by Ctein or other works on digital photography repair and retouching.

Anyone can learn to make simple adjustments to damaged photographs. If you are not interested in learning how to make complex repairs, a photo restoration firm can make your damaged images look almost new. Save this step for the images that are so faded or so broken that fixing them yourself may be nearly impossible without a lot of investment in time and effort, because digital restoration can be expensive.

Final File Preparation

The first step in the final preparation of your digital images is to create a backup that can be stored somewhere safely off site. A backup drive, a flash drive or a DVD can be given to another family member, or stored in a safe deposit box. It breaks my heart every time there is a natural disaster, not only for the lives that are lost or endangered and the property destroyed, but for the memories that cannot be recovered in a tangible way.

At this stage, you may not be ready to choose the final images for the book. And, you may have far more images than what you could possibly use, so the next step is to implement an organizational system that makes sense—not just for this book project, but for future projects.

For some, naming each digital image with the subject and approximate year will make sense. I have too many photographs to spend my time naming each image individually. I would rather keep folders within folders. My personal system is to keep images of families together, meaning that pictures of children will appear in the parent's file folder, but once the child is an adult, he or she receives his own folder. I organize by last name, then first name so that the file folders alphabetize well. I keep dated folders of events such as vacations or holiday celebrations so that there is a folder for each Thanksgiving by year, for example.

I also keep originals folders and work only from copies. I give my copies different file names with an indicator of what type of correction I have made. As an example, a file that has been color corrected will have its file name changed from IMG2036.jpg to IMG2036cc.jpg. That way, the files still alphabetize together but I can tell which is the original and which has been altered.

Consider adding borders to keep images with light skies, for example, from fading into the page, or adding photo corners to make the images look like they are in a scrapbook. There is no need to apply any final touches, however, until you are ready to place the images into the page layout.

Share

While you are scanning, share with other family members. Sharing will build interest in the book and may encourage family members to reciprocate with their photo treasures.

Send a few interesting images by email, post them on Facebook or Twitter, or add them to your family tree online. If you have a smart phone, send a few by Snapchat or Instragram. Create a few albums or slideshows at websites such as Photobucket (photobucket.com), or Flickr (www.flickr.com).

Sign up for one of the multitudes of online picture sharing sites such as Snapfish (www.snapfish.com), Shutterfly (www.shutterfly.com), or DotPhoto (www.dotphoto.com). Then send an announcement that you have created a photo album for them to see or order copies.

Create interesting gifts for purchase on sites such as CafePress (www.cafepress.com), or Zazzle (www.zazzle.com). If you are planning a reunion, photo gifts are popular.

You can even design your own fabric using photographs at websites such as Spoonflower (www.spoonflower.com), or Fabric on Demand (www.fabricondemand.com).

The primary goal for scanning is to create a digital image large enough and at the correct resolution to look good in your book. Once you have a print-quality digital image, you can reduce the image size for other uses such as sending by email or posting on the Internet.

A secondary goal while scanning is to preserve the photographic memories and documentary evidence of your family. Preserving your images is important, but try not to let the task of scanning sideline your book project. For those of you with hundreds or thousands of images to scan, it could.

Chapter 10

Cover Design for Print

If you have not given much thought to your book's title while you were writing, once you start designing the cover, you must. In fact, choosing the right title and making it look good on the cover may be the most difficult element of cover design. Fortunately, there is a fairly simple formula for the other elements expected on the front and back covers as well as on the spine.

Choosing a Good Title

The title will affect the perception readers have of the book and as such, the title should be the most prominent item on the cover. A non-fiction title is like a promise you are making to the reader for what they will experience reading the book. While it is tempting to use a title that is also a clever play on words (e.g. Deep Roots and Long Branches), if you want potential buyers to know which family you are writing about, it is best to be specific in the title or subtitle.

You could use "Descendants of ... " or "Ancestors of ... " or "The Unusual Lineage of ... " plus the names of the main characters, a time period or a region to distinguish your family from others with the same surname.

Most online bookstores will list both your title and subtitle in the short listings, so, if you prefer, you can use a shorter title followed by a more lengthy, explanatory subtitle.

The following are examples of good titles:

Up the Mississippi: The Laidlaw Family of England, New Orleans and Illinois

Descendants of Abial Washburn (1841-1899) and Susannah Cooke Washburn (1850-1919): From Georgia to Tennessee and Back

Handcarts Across the Plains: The Hubert Miller Family from Illinois (1830) to Oregon (1850)

These are not-so-good titles:
Our Family
The Third Generation
The Browns of Ohio

On the cover, typeset the title in a font large enough to be readable in a small thumbnail online. Online bookstores and eReaders will display your cover this way and often the small image is all a potential buyer has to evaluate the book.

Cover Layout Basics

How your cover is designed depends upon how it will be bound—hardbound, hardbound with a dustcover, or softbound (paperback).

A paperback cover is printed on a single sheet that wraps from the front around the spine to the back. It will be printed at a size larger than the book, then attached to the book with glue and trimmed so that the page and cover edges are smooth and even.

Hardbound covers can be made from either cloth or paper. They are glued to stiff boards to form a solid cover. A paper cover for a hardbound book will look like modern textbooks—full color with a glossy coating. Paper covers for hardbound books are designed even larger than those for softbound books because they must wrap around the edges of the boards and be glued down to form part of the inside cover. An endsheet will be glued over the edges of the cover.

Cloth covers are made of anything from linen to leather, depending upon how much you are willing to pay and the printer's equipment. Cloth covers, typically, do not have much more than the title and the author's name. Many cloth-covered books also have a full-color, paper dust jacket that wraps around the cloth cover. The dust jacket uses flaps inside the front and back covers to keep it secure.

Whether you are designing a paper cover or a dust jacket, your printer should have a template for you to follow. Many printers have template generators that will give you an exact size based upon the number of pages in the book, which will determine spine width. You can assemble the elements at any time, however, and create the final cover once you have a page count.

Cover templates will have three areas defined by the edge of the element: the bleed edge, the trim edge and the safe area.

The safe area is the innermost area that allows for any slippage when the printed cover is attached to the book's interior. Most templates will give you three safe areas, one each for the front cover, the back cover and the spine (the three shaded areas in the illustration). Notice that the safe areas are away from

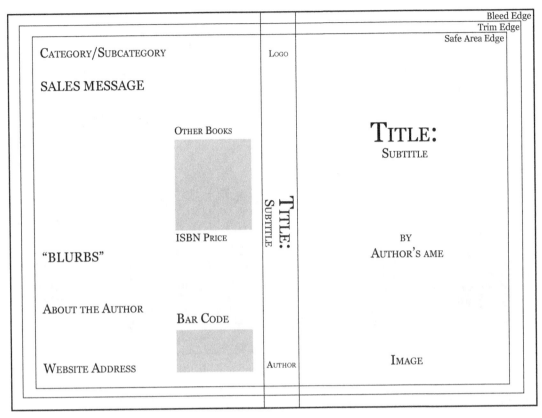

Cover elements.

the edges of the spine and the front and back covers. Keep all text, as well as the barcode, and any logo images within the safe areas.

The trim edge is where the book will be trimmed once the cover is applied to the interior pages so that the finished book will have clean, smooth edges.

The bleed edge is the area where photographs or solid background color should reach, so that when the book is trimmed, there is no danger of leaving a white line around an edge because nothing was printed in that area.

Cover Elements

Covers have three elements: the front, the spine, and the back. Most covers are designed in a single piece, and when laid flat, the front cover will be on the right-hand side, the spine in the middle and the back cover on the left.

If you use a print-on-demand printer that has an online cover generator—not a template but a design tool—you may be able to design the cover in three separate parts. Using one of these cover generators, however, will give you fewer options than designing it yourself.

If you design your own cover, create it as a single piece. You can use a word processor (although not ideal), an image editing program, a page layout program

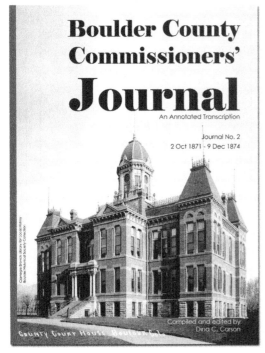 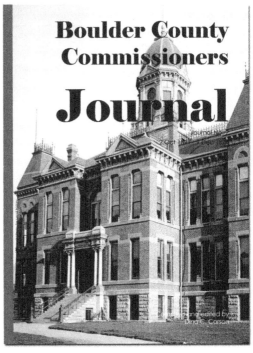

Cover photograph properly placed (left); Cover photograph making title difficult to read (right).

or a vector graphics editor such as Adobe Illustrator. One of the benefits of using a page layout program or a vector graphics editor is that they are built for creating cover files—to combine images with crisp, sharp type.

For ideas, take a look at Book Cover Archive (www.bookcoverarchive.com). This website offers a gallery of book covers created by professionals.

Front Cover

The front cover should get the reader's attention. The title should be the most prominent element on the cover, set in a font that is easy to read. The following are popular cover fonts: Baskerville, ChunkFive, Franchise, League Gothic, and Trajan.

For the background, use a photograph, a color, or a texture as long as the area where the title and subtitle are placed is plain (subtle) enough that the reader has no trouble reading the text at a glance. Avoid background elements that are too busy and those that do not create enough color contrast with the title text.

If you use an image, choose one that says something about the contents. The illustration shows two covers with the same title, but uses the background photograph in a different way. The key to making a book cover image look great is finding one that leaves a large, nearly-solid area where you can place the title in a contrasting color. The cover on the left has enough plain sky for the title and subtitle to be read clearly. The closeup cover image does not.

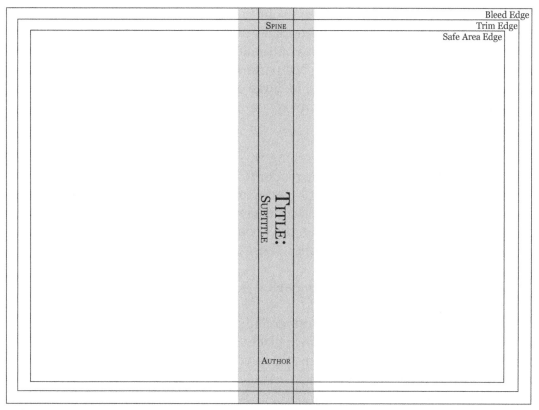

Spine wrap.

If you do not have an appropriate photograph in your own collection, you may be able to find a historic photograph that you could license, or you could purchase an image from one of the online rights-managed image companies for a few dollars.

Size and resolution matter and your cover image is likely to be the largest image you use for this project. The resolution should be 300 ppi at a size big enough to cover the bleed area. A cover with a 2.5" spine, for example, would measure 19.5" x 17.5" which is 5850 pixels by 5250 pixels.

If you cannot find the perfect photograph for the cover, blocks of color or subtle patterns also work.

The Spine

The spine will contain your title, your name as the author (full name, initials plus last name, or last name only), and a publishing company logo, if you have one.

The lettering on the spine goes from top to bottom—never the other way— so that all of the titles read the same way when books are spine out on the bookshelf.

The tricky part about designing the spine is making the elements (background image) stop at precisely the point at which the cover bends, either to the front or back. One way to avoid this is to use a solid color, a texture, or a photograph that continues across the entire cover. Another option is to create a spine wrap, where a graphic element or color continues onto the front and back covers to disguise a little slippage if the cover is not placed perfectly during production.

The typeface on the spine must be large and legible, and typically, the same one you used for the title on the front cover.

Back Cover

The back cover does most of the selling. It should explain why the reader will want your book and gently asks the reader to buy a copy.

If you have solicited blurbs or endorsements, your best endorsement(s) should go on the back cover. The back cover should include a bit about you as the author, or why you have written the book. If there are other books you have written, there may be room to mention those books, or to show their covers, page count, ISBNs and price.

If you have a website where the book is sold, the URL should appear prominently on the back cover.

If you plan to sell your book commercially through a print-on-demand printer (such as Lulu or Amazon), you must place an ISBN barcode at the bottom right corner about one quarter inch from the spine. The barcode can also include the price, although price is optional.

Some printers will include the barcode for you in their template. If you are using one of the ISBNs belonging to your print-on-demand printer, the barcode will be placed on the cover as you create it. If you are printing through an offset printer and must purchase an ISBN barcode, you can do so online. There are many companies offering barcodes for as little as $10. You will receive an .eps (EPS) image by email to use in your design. If you are purchasing your own ISBNs from the Bowker Company, they also offer barcodes for sale.

The other element you will need if you plan to sell your book to libraries or bookstores is a subject heading in the top left corner of the back cover. This is to give the librarians or bookstore employees an idea where to categorize the book.

Book Industry Standards Advisory Committee (BISAC) codes are the standard across the industry for subject headings. If you search online for BISAC codes, you will find a complete list. For most family histories, the code will be Reference/Genealogy. If you are using a print-on-demand printer, this question will come up as you are creating a listing for your book. Some printers make it easy to search for the BISAC code, others do not. Some printers allow you to list two or more categories, others do not. Search online for the complete list, then use the best subject heading on the back cover.

Advanced Cover Design

The following are additional tips for designing effective covers:

First, go to Amazon.com and take a look at Todd A. Stone's book, *Novelist's Boot Camp*. This is a simple cover, in two colors, black and army olive, but it says something about what is in the book, and does so simply.

Now take a look at *Virginia Historical Genealogies* by John Bennett Boddie. This is a black-and-white cover that is about as simple as is possible, but it does not re-produce well as a thumbnail on screen, does it? Arguably, this is a well-written book, but does the cover give you that impression? This book has been around for more than fifty years, so it is hard to be critical of a cover that was designed before major printing technology changes. However, the contents are deserving of a better cover.

Using Color

To make areas of solid black (such as your title text) look its best, use the formula for rich black, which is: 40% cyan, 40% magenta, 40% yellow, 100% black. You will notice that these are in CMYK colors. CMYK is the color palette most printers prefer. If you are designing your cover in your word processor or image editing program, you may not be able to choose the CMYK color palette, so the colors you are seeing on screen in the RGB palette may look slightly different when printed. Page layout and vector graphics programs are designed for working in CMYK.

Limit the cover's color palette to two or three colors and their various tints. That should be a sufficient variation unless you are using a photograph. If you are, choose colors from the photograph for other elements such as the subhead "About the Author" on the back cover. As with interior text, black text is still best for most elements on the cover.

If you need help choosing colors that look good together, use a good color picker. There are apps and online color wheels available, or buy one of Jim Krause's books, *Color Index*, or *Color Index 2*. If you want to go all out, buy one of the Pantone Color Guides (www.pantone.com).

Selecting great color combinations is not easy. If your spouse will not let you choose your own shirts, ask for help choosing colors for your book cover.

Other Cover Considerations

Once you have a cover design in mind, scale it down to a small thumbnail of one inch by one and a half inches (1" x 1.5"). This is how your cover will appear to people shopping at an online bookstore. A thumbnail image is how you will present the cover on your blog, website, Facebook, on a bookmark, or business card to give away to interested family members. If the title is not easy to read at the thumbnail size, then revise the cover for those uses with bigger, bolder text.

Save your cover in different sizes. You may need an eBook version (600 pixels x 800 pixels), an online bookstore version (Amazon's requirement is 1880 pixels x 2500 pixels), one for your blog or social media (400 pixels x 600 pixels), and a small thumbnail 90 pixels x 108 pixels (the standard cover size in Amazon's email promotions).

If you have plans for writing more than one book on the same family, consider using a branded look, that is, the same layout with different colors or photographs so that the books look like they belong together.

Your cover is the ambassador for your book. Some family members will want a copy even if it comes as loose leaf sheets wrapped in newspaper. Most readers, however, will form an impression of the book's contents by looking at the cover. When designing your cover, you should be able to find many suitable possibilities from the hundreds of thousands of non-fiction books already published. Use one as your guide. Bottom line: all of your hard work writing the book deserves to be covered in something beautiful, and representative of the quality of the contents.

Chapter 11

Final Files for Print

How you prepare your final files depends upon your printer. Most printers want PDF files because they are the least problematic. If you send a file in a word processing format such as Word, and you have used a font that the printer does not have, the text may re-format in a way you do not intend. By creating a PDF, there are rarely any font issues because the process of creating the PDF embeds the fonts into the document. Creating a PDF is, in some ways, like taking a snapshot of your manuscript. It will create a file that looks exactly like your manuscript file whether you created it in a word processing program or a page layout program. Most word processing and page layout software have the ability to save a document as a PDF.

Create Final PDFs

If you are using one of Adobe's software products to create your PDF (Acrobat or InDesign, for example), there are different PDF settings including press quality or high quality print (what we want for a printed book), smallest file size (appropriate for emailing the book), and several other settings in between. The best settings for printed material are: Press Quality, High Quality Printing or PDF/X 1a:2001. Most page layout programs will give you a choice in PDF settings, your word processor may not. In most cases, the printed book will still look fine.

If you use a digital or offset printer, ask for their preferred PDF settings before saving your files. Most print-on-demand printers, on the other hand, will accept whatever file you upload, so the responsibility for creating a file that will look its best when printed is up to you.

After creating the PDF, check it over carefully by comparing it to your original manuscript file to make sure nothing shifted or was lost in the conversion. If you are using a digital or offset printer, send a printed copy of your final manuscript along with the PDF files as a reference. Print-on-demand printers do not require this. They will use your files exactly as you send them.

Uploading Files for Print

If you have created your final layout in chapters so that they are easier to work with, it is safer to send the printer a single file so there is no chance the files could be printed out of order. Programs such as InDesign will take your individual files and combine them into a single book-length PDF. Adobe Acrobat will also combine individual PDF files into a larger book-length file.

If you must upload your manuscript files individually, the best way to make sure they are printed in the correct order is to begin each file name with a number so that the computer arranges them in the correct order. Unfortunately, if you number your files starting with a one (1), and you also have an eleven (11), the computer may order the files this way: 1, 11, 2.

The only way to avoid this is to count the total number of files, and use a sufficient number of zeros preceding the file number to force the computer to put the files in the correct order.

If there are fewer than ten files, there should be no issues, as the computer will number those files from one (1) to nine (9) in order. If there are ten or more files but fewer than one hundred, create two digit numbers from 01 to 09, so that subsequent numbers will be in the correct order. If there are more than one hundred files, file names require two zeros in front of the numbers from one (001) to nine (009), and a single zero before each and every number from ten (010) to ninety-nine (099). Numbers greater than one hundred will fall in order correctly.

Once you upload the files, the best way to see whether or not the files were placed in their proper order is to order a proof. Many print-on-demand printers offer a digital PDF proof for you to download. This should not cost you anything, but proofing on screen and proofing in print are different. You will catch different errors. It is worth the money to print a proof copy as well.

Examine the digital and print proofs carefully page by page. You may be surprised what you find. Missing punctuation and incorrectly applied styles are common errors. Watch for places where widows or orphans were created by text shift. It happens. Make sure your illustrations remain in place along with any captions or credits.

Chapter 12

Other Information about Your Book

Once you start the process of uploading files to a print-on-demand printer, requesting ISBNs or creating marketing materials for your book, you will need the following information. Keep it gathered in a convenient place so that you can cut and paste whatever is required of vendors or websites.

If you have purchased your own ISBNs, much of this information will inform the book buying community about your book. If you use a print-on-demand printer, they will ask for much of this information when you upload your files. Each printer has slightly different requirements. What follows is the information asked for most often.

Title

Title. Keep the title and subtitle separate.

Subtitle. Keep the title and subtitle separate.

Author and Publisher

Primary Author. List your name as the primary author. If you have co-authors or other contributors, you should have a chance to add their names as well.

Author Biography. Write a few paragraphs about yourself as the author and why you wrote the book.

Publisher. If you are acting as your own publisher, you have a choice whether to create a publishing company, or not. For tax and legal reasons you may wish to do so. One sign that you are a self-publisher, however, is naming the publishing company after yourself.

Language and Printing Location

Language. The primary language of the book.

Country. The country in which the book was published, not printed.

Important Dates

Copyright year. The year in which the book was finished. Although your copyright existed from the time you put pen to paper, most publishers use the most current year as the copyright date, so that readers know that the information is current.

Publication Date. This is a fictional date used by the publishing industry to schedule book reviews ahead of the book's official launch. Use the date when your book is available for sale.

Audience

Target Audience. Unless you are writing a children's book, the audience will always be Trade.

Metadata

Together, the title, license, description, category and keywords make up the metadata—cataloging information about your book that is key to book sales. Any mis-matches in the metadata will make it difficult for the big databases (online book catalogues) to place your book in front of the right potential buyers.

License. Indicate that you own the copyright to your work, that you are not re-packaging a work already in the public domain.

Description. This is your sales language, your chance to interest potential readers. Some sites use descriptions as short as 200 characters, others as long as 4000. Have several descriptions ready with the most important information wrapped up in the shortest description, and additional detail in the longer descriptions. If you want to sell your book, the description may be one of your most important marketing tools. Lulu describes "providing too little detail in the description" as the greatest mistake of new authors.

Category. Many printers will use the BISAC codes, others have a search option, still others make it as confusing as humanly possible. When in doubt, if Genealogy is not a main category, look for Reference/Genealogy & Heraldry. A secondary category could be History (U.S. History, European History, etc.) plus the local area where the book takes place (U.S. History/Midwest).

Keywords. Most sites allow five or more keyword phrases separated by commas. Choose the five most important and put those first. For example, Campbell Family History, Campbell Genealogy, Abraham Campbell Family, Campbell Family Kentucky, Campbell Family Ohio. If you are able to add more keyword phrases, do. More keywords will help potential readers find the book. For most family histories, the keywords should be about the surname and the location(s) where the family lived. Think of the phrases another researcher interested in the family would use to find the book. There are keyword search programs online that can help with this, such as Google Adwords Keyword Planner (adwords.google.com). This tool is free, but you must create an account to use it.

ISBN and Price

ISBN. If you have your own ISBN, use it. If you do not, leave this blank and the printer will assign one of theirs to you.

Price. Choose a price higher than the wholesale price if you want to make money each time the book is sold. Another reason you may wish to choose a price higher than the wholesale price is to give the distributor (printer) the opportunity to price the book at a discount. Book buyers love bargains, but if you price the book at the wholesale cost, the distributor cannot sell the book for less than what it costs to manufacture it.

The following are a few items particular to Amazon (CreateSpace), Lulu and Bowker (the ISBN Agency).

Amazon (CreateSpace)

Distribution. Amazon offers the following outlets for distribution: Amazon.com, Amazon Europe, Create Space eStore, Bookstores and Online Retailers, CreateSpace Direct. If you are using one of their ISBNs your book is also eligible for distribution to libraries and academic institutions—a plus for Reference/Genealogy books.

Prices. If you have chosen distribution outside of the United States, choose US Dollars, Euros, and British Pounds. Google's online currency calculator can help convert U.S. dollars to English pounds or euros. Round the prices up to the nearest .99 or .95, as prices ending that way have become customary.

Option to Publish on Kindle. If you use CreateSpace to publish your print book they will give you the option to create a Kindle version.

Lulu

Private Access. One of my favorite features of Lulu is that you can publish a book and keep it completely private, meaning that only you can order copies. This is appropriate for books that you may wish to distribute to family members that have information about living people you would not want distributed outside the family.

Direct Access. Direct Access gives you a private URL to direct family members to buy the book for themselves. This option gives you less control over distribution than private access, but it is a good option if you have family spread out all over the country, and you want them to be able to buy their own copies and have the books delivered directly to them.

General Access. Any book you assign as general access will become available through Lulu's catalog as well as the Amazon catalog.

Bowker Company (ISBN Agency)

ISBN 10. Older ISBNs had only 10 digits. If you have a newer ISBN it will have 13 digits, and there is a calculator on the site to convert it to the older 10 digit version. This site asks for both, and checks one against the other for accuracy.

ISBN 13. The ISBN for your book.

LCCC. A Library of Congress Catalog Number.

Medium. Medium is the format of the book, usually print or eBook, unless you have chosen to distribute it as an audiobook, or on CD or DVD instead.

Format. In most cases the format will be paperback or hardbound.

Title Status. If you want the book industry to know that your book is available for sale, use Active. You can use the term Forthcoming, if you are months away from publishing. Be sure, however, to come back and change the status. The big databases that the book sellers use will show the book as unavailable until you change the status to Active.

Price Type. Choose Retail Price.

Keep a file with this information gathered in one place. When you are ready to let others know that you have a book available, having these details handy will save time.

Section 3

If you have skipped over the section on print publishing because you only wish to publish in an electronic format, I encourage you to do both. Formatting for print takes more time than formatting directly for eBooks, however, the conversion of your manuscript files once you have a print file is fairly easy.

There is a more important reason to consider print, however, and that is to make sure you send a printed copy of your book—your hard work—to the major genealogical collections around the country:

The Library of Congress
The Family History Library at Salt Lake City, Utah
The DAR Library in Washington, D.C.
The Denver Public Library
The Allen County Library in Fort Wayne, Indiana
The Midwest Genealogy Center in Independence, MO
The New York Public Library

Include on your list, local libraries in the places where your ancestors lived.

Besides the benefit of contributing to libraries, your electronic book may cease to exist in a few years, because electronic formats come and go. Consider the Atari and Wang computers, not to mention the 8-Track tape and the Betamax.

Natural disasters occur. Computers crash.

Besides, researchers in other locations may be interested in your work. The next person who takes up your family line may be a generation or two away. Please, give consideration to a print version of your book.

The goal for this section on electronic publishing is to help you take what you prepared for print, and convert it into an electronic edition of your book. Much of the advice about preparing your manuscript for print, applies to preparing it for an eBook. The differences are what follow.

Chapter 13

Converting a Print Manuscript to eBook Formats

Most print-on-demand printers will offer to convert your print files to electronic versions appropriate for eBooks. Some readers will prefer the book in an electronic format making it worth the effort to convert it. However, if you have not prepared your manuscript as an electronic book, the results may not look good.

EBook readers allow the text to re-flow according to the reader's wishes. The reader can decide how large or small to make the font, which means how much text will appear on each screen will change.

Converting your print-book PDF to an electronic format can be problematic. The strength of PDFs is their ability to keep the text formatted *exactly* as you want it. The problem then becomes undoing all of that formatting to create flowing text. Many eBook aggregators (companies that will make your book available in many different formats for different types of eReaders) and print-on-demand printers will not accept PDFs for conversion to eBook formats. They would rather have the text in Word, XML, HTML or EPUB (the format used by the iPad, iPhone, Nook and Sony).

Most word processors allow you to save your file as either XML or HTML, but if the eBook aggregator or printer will take your native word processing file, so much the better.

Formatting for eBook Readers

When formatting a book for an eReader, the text must flow as one, long, continuous file and should follow a few formatting conventions.

Main Elements

Set up the manuscript for 8.5" x 11" pages. Your manuscript files cannot have any headers or footers which means no running headers with the book title or chapter title and no page numbers. The text must run in a single column, so remove columns from your layout.

Use a single, universal font in the same size throughout the book. Times New Roman is a good universal font and 12 points is the most common size. Use "Select All" (Control + A on the PC) to highlight all of the text in the file, then change the font to Times New Roman at 12 points.

Remove any hard breaks such as page breaks or section breaks. You may have to search for these by scrolling all the way through the manuscript.

If you use bullets, use only standard, round bullets. Replace any fancy bullets in your manuscript.

Reorder Non-essential Elements

Many eBook sellers offer readers a sample before they buy. Because of this, consider moving some items that belong in the front matter in a printed book, into the back matter of the eBook so that the reader can get a feel for the main body of the book in the sample. Some publishers are even moving the copyright information to the back. Anything you think is not essential to the beginning of the story, can be moved. The only exception is any front matter section that the reader needs for explanation prior to beginning the book such as your Author's Note or Methods.

Rename Chapters

If you have used chapter titles, re-name the chapters using simple Arabic numerals (e.g. Chapter 1, Chapter 2, etc.) before the chapter title. Most eBook conversion software will build a table of contents from the text in your files—submit your Table of Contents anyway. Change the chapter titles as above and remove the page numbers. Your printer or eBook aggregator will edit out what they do not need, and create links to the sections from the remaining Table of Contents.

Image Size

When converting a print-ready manuscript to an eBook, replace the full-resolution images with web-ready images (see Image Basics for eBooks). Smaller images will keep the download time short and the file size for the eBook small.

Image Placement

Images cannot be placed in a fixed spot on the page in an eBook. Images in eBooks must be placed in line with the text. To place the image correctly, when you reach the end of a paragraph, use a single return, then insert the image.

Insert another single return after the image followed by any accompanying caption and permissions. Use another single return and resume with the next paragraph.

Image Basics for eBook Readers

The same general guidelines apply when preparing images for eBooks as for print. Scan high enough to use the image in print or as a photographic gift. Then, alter the image in physical size and resolution for optimal use in an eBook.

Your goal in creating images for your eBook is to keep the overall book size down so that the download time is quick, while maintaining the quality of the images. This can be tricky, especially if your book contains many images.

The Kindle eReader, for example, only displays images in black-and-white, but other editions, such as the Kindle Fire, display images in full color. Use full-color images in your eBooks even though the file sizes may be greater than for black-and-white images. Tablets and smart phones display images in color. Save images in either the RGB or—for black-and-white original images—gray-scale color space.

Physical Size

First, adjust the physical size of the image in your image editing program. The ideal size for book cover images or full-screen-page images for the Kindle, for example, is 600 pixels x 800 pixels. First Edition Design Publishing, an eBook aggregator, suggests that most images be no more than 300 pixels tall. Reduce your image to a size that is within the limits, but not so small that the reader cannot figure out what the image is supposed to be. If necessary, crop the image first, to save file space.

The simplest way to convert the image from your print book files is to make a copy of your full-resolution images and place them in a different folder so that there is no possibility of overwriting the full-resolution images.

Further separate the images by the ones you want to display at full-screen size and those that can be displayed smaller. Use the batch function in your image-editing software to resize the images you want to occupy a full-screen to 600 x 800 pixels, and the smaller images to 300 pixels tall.

Resolution

Next, reduce the resolution of the images. Reducing the resolution to 72 ppi (screen resolution) will help keep each image under 100KB. There are a couple of ways to do this. Using your image editing program, you can reduce the resolution to 72 ppi, or some programs such as Photoshop (and Photoshop Elements) have a "save for the web" feature that provides options for different quality levels while saving. Photoshop has a 4-up preview setting that shows the original image, followed by images of three different levels of quality. Choose the setting that looks the best while making the file size smaller. I often achieve better results using the "save for the web" option than changing the resolution to 72 ppi directly.

File Format

Finally, save the image as a .jpg or .png if the image is a photograph or as a .gif or .png if the image is line art or an illustration. PNG images tend to be larger in file size, so JPG is often better for photographs, whereas PNG is often better for line art because the image quality is noticeably better than GIF.

Animation

Avoid animated graphics such as animated GIFs within your eBook files. Most dedicated eBook readers do not display animations. When these files are processed by the eBook distributor, the first image in the animation will be chosen as the final image. Stick with non-animated images unless you are creating an interactive eBook. More about interactivity shortly.

Screen Captures

Screen captures are less complicated to prepare for an eBook than for a print book. Your original screen capture will already be at screen resolution (72 ppi). Crop and edit as needed, then change the physical size to fit the intended use. (See more about recommendations for image sizes in eBooks, below.)

Book Cover Image

Adjust your book cover image before you convert it to a size appropriate for an eReader. Only the front cover will be shown, so copy the elements from your print cover file to a new document and remove anything too small to be read at 600 pixels x 800 pixels. Increase the size of your title, subtitle and author's name so that they can be clearly read in the smaller image. Because readers will judge whether they want to purchase based upon what they see on the cover, this is the one image you should leave at full-resolution (300 ppi). Having one full-resolution image will not increase the file size of the book enough to be a problem.

Formatting eBooks in HTML

Another way to create an electronic book from your manuscript files is to convert them to HTML. Many eBook aggregators will accept files in HTML. HTML files are, essentially, web pages. If you are thinking about publishing online, this is one way to convert your files into web-ready pages. (To make your manuscript HTML files look their best as a website, see Section 4: Publishing Online.)

File Conversion

Some word processing programs will convert their native files to HTML. Often, there is more than one choice for how the files are converted, including a Single File Web Page (.mht or .mhtml), a Web Page (.htm or .html), and a Web Page, Filtered (.htm or .html). Choose the Web Page optionif you want to use the HTML later to publish as a website.

When choosing the Web Page option, as the conversion takes place, the computer will create a file folder with the same name as the document (e.g. Chapter 1), and will take any images that were in the document, number them in the order that they were found, and place them in the file folder along with a link to the appropriate place in the text.

Formatting

During the conversion, your word processor will remove all headers, footers and columns and will place images in line with the text. This is exactly what an eBook aggregator will want.

What the word processor does not do, however, is convert the type into the same font at the same size. You will achieve more consistent results if you change the font in your word processor before you convert the file to HTML.

Links

During the conversion, your word processor should create relative links from the images in the folder to the place where the images display in the HTML file. This is important, because as long as the HTML file and the folder with the images are kept together (not moved into different folders), the links will remain intact.

A hard link, on the other hand, is a specific place on your computer's hard drive. Once the eBook leaves your computer, the HTML file will not be able to find images using hard links.

A relative link looks like this:
< img src: "images/image1.jpg">

A hard link looks like this:
< img src: "C:\mydocuments\manuscript\images\image1.jpg">

One way to keep files with relative links together is to create a .zip folder that will hold all of your HTML files and the file folders with the images.

Testing Links

To test how the manuscript files were converted, first change the name of the folder holding the HTML files and the image folders (e.g. change the folder name from Manuscript to HTMLtest). Then use your web browser to open each of the HTML files. If relative links were created correctly, images should display correctly. If, however, you see a square with a big red ex (X) where an image should be, then the link to the image is broken.

You could convert the file again to make sure there was no problem during conversion, or you may need to open each file in an HTML editor to fix the broken links. You will find all manner of HTML editors from free online downloads to the sophisticated (and expensive) Dreamweaver by Adobe.

Set Yourself Up to Self-Publish

There is no doubt that most members of your family will want a print copy of your book. Once your print manuscript is complete, however, the changes necessary to make those files compatible with tablets and eReaders is not difficult. Since approximately twenty-five percent of all adults (and an even higher percentage of children) have made the leap to electronic devices on which to read books, converting your print manuscript to an eBook edition will be appreciated.

Chapter 14

Converting a Print Manuscript to a PDF for the Screen

Another way to create an electronic book is to create a PDF meant to be read on a computer or tablet screen. PDFs created this way are easily distributed by email or a file-sharing service such as Dropbox.

Page Layout

The rules for formatting these books, fortunately, are similar to the rules for formatting your print book, with one major exception—these books should not be set up with left and right pages. These PDFs are read as single pages, so you do not want the text to appear to jump back and forth as the reader moves to each new page. The margins for left and right pages are different in a print book, but in a PDF meant to be read on screen, the margins should be the equal and wider. Typical margins for an 8.5" x 11" PDF eBook are: top—2"–2.5"; sides—1"; bottom—1" if the page numbers are placed in the header, or 1.25" if the page numbers are in the footer.

Type Size

The type should also be a bit bigger than your print edition, and spread out a little bit more to make reading on screen easier. Point sizes of 12 or 13 are common for this use, with line leading at 14 or 15 points. Headlines and subheads should also be larger.

You may have to move the illustrations around a bit as the text changes due to the increased margins and type size.

6 Book Title		Chapter Title 7
Lorem ipsum dolor sit amet, consectetur adipisicing elit, sed do eiusmod tempor incididunt ut labore et dolore magna aliqua. Ut enim ad minim veniam, quis nostrud exercitation ullamco laboris nisi ut aliquip ex ea commodo consequat. Duis aute irure dolor in reprehenderit in voluptate velit esse cillum dolore eu fugiat nulla pariatur. Excepteur sint occaecat cupidatat non proident, sunt in culpa qui officia deserunt mollit anim id est laborum.		Lorem ipsum dolor sit amet, consectetur adipisicing elit, sed do eiusmod tempor incididunt ut labore et dolore magna aliqua. Ut enim ad minim veniam, quis nostrud exercitation ullamco laboris nisi ut aliquip ex ea commodo consequat. Duis aute irure dolor in reprehenderit in voluptate velit esse cillum dolore eu fugiat nulla pariatur. Excepteur sint occaecat cupidatat non proident, sunt in culpa qui officia deserunt mollit anim id est laborum.

Headline Headline Headline

Lorem ipsum dolor sit amet, consectetur adipisicing elit, sed do eiusmod tempor incididunt ut labore et dolore magna aliqua. Ut enim ad minim veniam, quis nostrud exercitation ullamco laboris nisi ut aliquip ex ea commodo consequat. Duis aute irure dolor in reprehenderit in voluptate velit esse cillum dolore eu fugiat nulla pariatur. Excepteur sint occaecat cupidatat non proident, sunt in culpa qui officia deserunt mollit anim id est laborum.

Headline Headline Headline

Lorem ipsum dolor sit amet, consectetur adipisicing elit, sed do eiusmod tempor incididunt ut labore et dolore magna aliqua. Ut enim ad minim veniam, quis nostrud exercitation ullamco laboris nisi ut aliquip ex ea commodo consequat. Duis aute irure dolor in reprehenderit in voluptate velit esse cillum dolore eu fugiat nulla pariatur. Excepteur sint occaecat cupidatat non proident, sunt in culpa qui officia deserunt mollit anim id est laborum.

Lorem ipsum dolor sit amet, consectetur adipisicing elit, sed do eiusmod tempor incididunt ut labore et dolore magna aliqua. Ut enim ad minim veniam, quis nostrud exercitation ullamco laboris nisi ut aliquip ex ea commodo consequat. Duis aute irure dolor in reprehenderit in voluptate velit esse cillum dolore eu fugiat nulla

Lorem ipsum dolor sit amet, consectetur adipisicing elit, sed do eiusmod tempor incididunt ut labore et dolore magna aliqua. Ut enim ad minim veniam, quis nostrud exercitation ullamco laboris nisi ut aliquip ex ea commodo consequat. Duis aute irure dolor in reprehenderit in voluptate velit esse cillum dolore eu fugiat nulla pariatur. Excepteur sint occaecat cupidatat non proident, sunt in culpa qui officia deserunt mollit anim id est laborum.

Headline Headline Headline

Lorem ipsum dolor sit amet, consectetur adipisicing elit, sed do eiusmod tempor incididunt ut labore et dolore magna aliqua. Ut enim ad minim veniam, quis nostrud exercitation ullamco laboris nisi ut aliquip ex ea commodo consequat. Duis aute irure dolor in reprehenderit in voluptate velit esse cillum dolore eu fugiat nulla pariatur. Excepteur sint occaecat cupidatat non proident, sunt in culpa qui officia deserunt mollit anim id est laborum.

Headline Headline Headline

Lorem ipsum dolor sit amet, consectetur adipisicing elit, sed do eiusmod tempor incididunt ut

Manuscript typeset for print (left); Manuscript typeset for PDF (right).

Page Size

If you created the printed book at 6" x 9" or 7" x 10," increase the page size to 8.5" x 11." In the event the reader wants to print out a page or two, it will print on standard U.S. paper.

On the other hand, one of the great advantages to electronic books is that you are not limited to the common page sizes used by book printers. If you book looks best as a landscape, then landscape it. If it looks best tall and skinny, go tall and skinny. Okay, perhaps not tall and skinny. Stick to the rules of readability for the reader's sake, but if your creative side is itching to use an innovative grid, give it a try. In fact, magazines often pioneer creative layouts without sacrificing readability.

Hyperlinks

Another advantage to electronic books is the ability to provide live links to resources on the internet. That means, you could use thumbnails of images in your PDF book with links to full-size images you maintain at a photo-sharing site online such as Flickr. Or, you can increase the number of images you wish to share with readers by giving them a link to a gallery of images you maintain online.

Include links to the repositories where you found sources, or interesting places you visited while researching. The possibilities for resource links are endless.

PDF Security

One disadvantage to creating a PDF book is the inability to limit distribution. You are able to change the security settings within a PDF so that recipients are not able to print or must use a password to open the file. There are also software programs that will electronically mark a PDF so that you can trace the original recipient. In practical terms, however, once the book is distributed as a PDF, it can be shared. If your book is a labor of love to share with as many people as are interested, then easy distribution is a plus and security is not a big concern.

Book Cover Image

Use a book cover image as the first page of your PDF book. When readers look on their tablets or in folders on their desktops, the icon they will see is the book's cover. A good book cover image is the easiest way to distinguish one PDF file from another. Take a look at the front cover you designed for your print book. Take the elements from the front cover and copy them to a new file with the same paper size as your PDF. If anything, you want your title and subtitle to be even more prominent in this version than in the print version since it will be seen as a small icon.

One reason PDFs are so attractive is that they are so easy to create and distribute. Once your print manuscript is ready, most printers will prefer a PDF. So why go to the trouble of converting that printer-ready PDF to one meant for reading on screen? The most compelling reason is to make it easier for the reader to read the book from a computer monitor or tablet, and the steps you must take to covert the manuscript are not difficult.

Chapter 15

Interactivity for eBooks

One of the best features of tablets such as the iPad is the interactivity possible in books designed for these devices. Interactivity, of course, is the hallmark of the Internet, so everything in this section about interactivity in eBooks applies to books published online.

Interactivity Options

Interactivity is not just for entertaining children, it enriches the reader's experience if they can click on an audio file and hear a relative tell a story, or click on an animation to see how a blacksmith created tools in the 19th Century. Even simple interactivity such as the ability to jump from section to section within the book makes the book easier to use.

Interior Links

Create a detailed Table of Contents containing not only the names of chapters and sections, but each headline and subhead. Then, link the Table of Contents to the appropriate place. Create links to footnotes or endnotes, as well.

Exterior Links

Link to resources on the Internet. Link to a gallery of photographs you keep on Flickr or a site where you have prints for sale, for example. Link to a website where you have more family information, to your blog or social media, or to a web form where readers can give you feedback. You could connect with other researchers this way.

Post full-size images in a photo gallery online, and use thumbnails in the book. Link the thumbnails to the full-sized images.

Some URLs you may want to link to are so long that they look daunting in the text. You can create custom URLs that are far shorter by using Bitly (www.bitly.com), or Goo.gl (goo.gl).

Rich Media

Your readers will be truly amazed if you add video, audio, 3D or flash animation. Use audio of interviews with family members or video of family reunions. You may be able to find additional audio, video or animation online without copyright restriction, or that you could license for use in your interactive book. There are so many possibilities: period music, battlefield sounds, animation of a barn raising, video of a re-enactment. If you need inspiration, take a look at the series, *The Civil War* by Ken Burns. He is a master at combining images, video and audio.

Widgets

Some eBook creating software, such as iBook Author, allow you to add widgets. Widgets are small computer programs that perform specific tasks. Some genealogical possibilities include: age calculator (85 years, 6 months, 3 days becomes 3 December 1848); relationship calculator (who the ancestor is to you—2nd cousins once removed); live mapping (showing an online map based upon a mention of a place in the text), and so on. Clever coders are creating an abundance of new widgets every day.

Interactivity Software

The following are some of the software options to add rich media to your manuscript files. You may find much more on open source code sites on the Internet.

Adobe Acrobat

If you are creating a PDF version of your book, the full program Acrobat (not the free reader) (www.adobe.com), will allow you to add video, audio, and animations.

iBooks Author

iBooks Author is a Mac-platform tool (www.apple.com/ibooks-author/), for creating interactive books for the iBook app, available for the iPad and iPhone. This software has built-in widgets that you can drag and drop into the text, as well as accessibility options for people who are vision impaired. The software will create an audio version for those readers. iBook Author will also lead you through the process of making the book available on iTunes.

InDesign

Many magazines are using InDesign (www.adobe.com), to create interactive content in their digital editions. You can add rich media, page transitions and time the start and stop of animations on each page. You can also create liquid layouts so that the page will re-format if the user turns the tablet from portrait (upright) to landscape (sideways). Once completed, these books are saved to a flash animation format that can be read in most web browsers.

QuarkXPress

QuarkXPress (www.quark.com), allows you to create interactive content especially for the Blio eReader. You can add slideshows, video and content from web pages with embedded HTML. Once you are ready to publish, you can submit your book to the Blio bookstore which is powered by Baker&Taylor, one of the largest distributors of books in the United States.

PowerPoint

Although used mostly for presentations, PowerPoint can also be used for publishing interactive books. In addition to audio and video, it offers page transitions, and animated text and shapes. Microsoft makes a PowerPoint Viewer so that the people you share the book with, can view it. Download it free in the Download Center at Microsoft (www.microsoft.com).

Apps

There are applications (apps) to create interactive books from your tablet, such as the following for iPad and iPhone—Book Creator, Story Creator, Halftone 2 Graphic Novel Creator (www.itunes.com); and these for the Android platform—Book Creator and Touchoo (play.google.com).

There are more apps coming along every day. Your ability to share your book depends upon the app.

If you want to take the next step up in electronic publishing, add some interactivity. Digitize your old home movies or audio tapes and link the digital files to the action in the book. Search the Internet for animation or video of how an ancestor may have worked or lived. Study the techniques used to create good documentaries and use them in your interactive book.

SECTION 4

In the section entitled Online Production Basics, we discussed the different places you could host (publish) your book online. Using Google Books, you can give readers the experience of reading a book using a web browser, but viewing the pages in side-by-side spreads more like reading a printed book. You can post the contents in snippets on a blog, social media such as Facebook, as stories linked to your tree on one of the major genealogy websites, or on your own website.

The goal for this publishing online section is to help you convert your print manuscript to a website, a blog or social media.

Chapter 16

Converting a Print Manuscript to a Website

While it is possible for you to convert your manuscript files directly into HTML from some word processing programs, your book will look much better if you use an HTML editor to build an interactive book online. HTML is not the only computer language in which to create a website, either. There are many others, but I am only going to describe the process of converting your manuscript files into HTML here. In addition to the software needed to build the site, you will also need a few Internet services.

Creating Your Own Website

In order to create your own website, you need a domain name, a web host with server space to hold your website files, a way to build the website, and a method of sending the files to the server.

Domain Name

A domain name (also called a URL—Uniform Resource Locator) is the address where web browsers will locate your website in order to display it. Google's domain name, for example, is www.google.com. If you know a company's domain name, you can type it directly into the search bar.

You can obtain your own URL through one of the many registrars online, such as: Register.com (www.register.com) or Domain.com (www.domain.com). Registering a domain name will cost anywhere from a few dollars per year to about twenty-five dollars per year. If you stop paying the fee, you will lose the domain and Internet users will no longer be able to find your website.

Web Hosting

The files that make up your website must sit on a server (computer) that is connected to the Internet all the time.

You can obtain free server space for a website. The most popular free website hosts are: Weebly (www.weebly.com), and Wix (www.wix.com). There are hundreds of others. Free sites often include a domain name, although, it may be a subdomain of the company, such as: www.yourname.webhostingcompany.com.

Many free website hosts offer simple HTML editing tools to help you create a website. How much control you will have over the look and the organization, depends upon the type of tools offered. Free sites often place advertising on your web pages. Some free sites limit the number of pages you can create. Others limit server space (often impacting the number of images you can use on the website) or traffic (the number of people visiting the site at a time and in a single month). Free is fantastic, as long as the company stays in business.

Another option is to purchase hosting for your website from an Internet Service Provider (ISP). Three of the biggest ISPs are HostGator (www.hostgator.com), NetworkSolutions (www.networksolutions.com) and GoDaddy (www.godaddy.com). There are also thousands of local and regional ISPs offering services at all price ranges.

Some ISPs offer web-building tools, many of which are drag and drop which means you do not need to know much about creating websites in order to use them. Most ISPs charge for a certain amount of server space before you have to buy more if you have many large files, such as video. Some ISPs also charge for traffic, so if you have a popular website, you may pay more for the number of people visiting the site. Most ISPs allow a generous amount of space and traffic in their basic (least expensive) packages.

HTML Editor

If you do not have the option of using your ISP's website building tools, or want to have more control over the look and contents of your website, you will need a way to build it. The most common way to build a site is in the computer coding language HTML using an HTML editor. HTML editors come in all levels of sophistication and price from free downloads found on the Internet to Adobe Dreamweaver (www.adobe.com).

For the most part, you do not need the most sophisticated program available to host your book as a website.

Uploading Files

If you build a website using an HTML editor, you must upload your files to the server space reserved for your site by your Internet Service Provider. Some ISPs have FTP (file transfer protocol) tools available from your account dashboard. Others will give you an FTP address and you must use an FTP program to upload files from your computer to the ISP's server. One of the most popular FTP programs is WS_FTP Pro (www.ipswitchft.com).

Building a Website

Earlier we discussed converting your manuscript files to HTML in order to submit the book to an eBook aggregator. If you have converted your manuscript files to HTML, you already have the building blocks for a website. The text and images are in place chapter by chapter through the book. What remains is to create a home page with links to each of the chapter files. That is one option. Another option would be to start from scratch. Whichever you choose, the following principals are the same.

Organizing the website well is key. At a glance, readers should be able to look at the home page and understand what to do next. Readers will want to know how to move through the book from beginning to end, without missing anything or becoming confused about where they are in the book.

Banner Images

Most websites use a banner at the top to identify the website, display a logo, and tell viewers what the website is about. Use the banner to show your book cover and give the title, subtitle and your name as the author.

Navigation

Every page of the website should have essential navigation, so that readers can go from place to place within the website without losing track of where they are, and without having to use the back button on their web browser repeatedly to access other sections of the website.

Place the essential navigation in a vertical column down the left-hand side of the website, rather than across the top unless you have very few chapters. The top area, if used for navigation, becomes crowded quickly or else you must use multiple rows of navigation which is difficult to read.

In the example (left), you will see that I have moved some of the front matter down farther in the navigation, so that readers can jump right in to the story.

Website Real Estate

The example on the next page shows three columns. I have used the left-hand column for the navigation because website viewers have come to expect the navigation on the left rather than on the right. I have kept the width of the center column (where the main text is) narrow enough to make reading easy. The rules of readability apply to online books as well as printed books. The right-hand column is reserved for thumbnails of images, links to other websites, or links to video or audio files.

BOOK COVER THUMBNAIL	**TITLE:** **SUBTITLE** BY **AUTHOR**	BANNER AREA

NAVIGATION

Home
Foreword
Introduction
Chapter 1
Chapter 2
Chapter 3
Chapter 4
Copyrights
Acknowledgments
Endnotes
Bibliography
Appendix A

HEADLINE

Lorem ipsum dolor sit amet, consectetur adipisicing elit, sed do eiusmod tempor incididunt ut labore et dolore magna aliqua. Ut enim ad minim veniam, quis nostrud exercitation ullamco laboris nisi ut aliquip ex ea commodo consequat. Duis aute irure dolor in reprehenderit in voluptate velit esse cillum dolore eu fugiat nulla pariatur. Excepteur sint occaecat cupidatat non proident, sunt in culpa qui officia deserunt mollit anim id est laborum.

PHOTOGRAPHS
ILLUSTRATIONS
AUDIO FILES
VIDEO FILES
LINKS

Organizing a book as a website.

Most websites are wider than they are tall to keep viewers from having to scroll down. It may not be possible for you break up the text into segments small enough to keep readers from having to scroll at all. Having to move from page to page a paragraph at a time is not much better than scrolling. Whether you let the readers scroll or create multiple pages is a balancing act.

Organization

One way to break up chapters into shorter sections, is to use subheads along with sub-navigation, and some "bread crumb" navigation so that readers always know where they are in the website. (See the example on the previous page.)

In order to give the reader a way to go on to the next section, you can put a "next" link at the end of each page, or you can create a navigation page for each chapter with each of the headlines and subheads linked to the appropriate text.

Index

Websites are searchable, so you do not need an index. Users can search a single web page using the Find tool on their web browsers. Searching throughout an en-

BOOK COVER THUMBNAIL	TITLE: SUBTITLE BY AUTHOR	
		BANNER AREA

Chapter 1 > The Wilsons Move West > June 1856

NAVIGATION

Home
Foreword
Introduction
Chapter 1
Chapter 2
Chapter 3
Chapter 4
Copyrights
Acknowledgments
Endnotes
Bibliography
Appendix A

JUNE 1856

Lorem ipsum dolor sit amet, consectetur adipisicing elit, sed do eiusmod tempor incididunt ut labore et dolore magna aliqua. Ut enim ad minim veniam, quis nostrud exercitation ullamco laboris nisi ut aliquip ex ea commodo consequat. Duis aute irure dolor in reprehenderit in voluptate velit esse cillum dolore eu fugiat nulla pariatur. Excepteur sint occaecat cupidatat non proident, sunt in culpa qui officia deserunt mollit anim id est laborum.

NEXT

PHOTOGRAPHS
ILLUSTRATIONS
AUDIO FILES
VIDEO FILES
LINKS

Website design using sub-navigation (bread crumb navigation).

tire website is a little more difficult unless you install a search function to do so. If you do not install a search function, create a sitemap containing the names of the key individuals along with their birth and death dates, and a link to the place where each individual's story begins.

Image Basics Online

Preparing images to use on the Internet is similar to preparing them for an eBook, with one major exception. The goal for placing images into an eBook is to keep the file size under 100 KB each. On the Internet, to keep pages loading quickly, thumbnail images are often used to keep the file sizes small. But you can use the thumbnail sized images as links to full-sized images so that readers have the option of looking at a document, for example, at full size or downloading an image for themselves. Full-sized images can be used to order prints, as well.

Linking to full-sized images is one distinct advantage publishing a book on the Internet has over eBooks. If your thumbnails are linked to larger images, explain that somewhere on the home page. Not everyone will understand that

```
┌─────────────────────────────────────────────────────────────┐
│ ┌───────────┐   TITLE:                                       │
│ │ BOOK      │                                                │
│ │ COVER     │   SUBTITLE                                     │
│ │ THUMBNAIL │                                                │
│ │           │   BY AUTHOR                                    │
│ └───────────┘                          BANNER AREA           │
├─────────────────────────────────────────────────────────────┤
│                                                              │
│  NAVIGATION        CHAPTER 1          ┌─────────────────┐    │
│                    Land in Missouri   │ PHOTOGRAPHS     │    │
│  Home                 Settling Down   │ ILLUSTRATIONS   │    │
│  Foreword             Building a Home │ AUDIO FILES     │    │
│  Introduction         Working the Land│ VIDEO FILES     │    │
│  Chapter 1         Economic Collapse  │ LINKS           │    │
│  Chapter 2            1856 Crop Failure                      │
│  Chapter 3            1857 Bank Failures                     │
│  Chapter 4         The Wilsons Move West                     │
│  Copyrights           June 1859                              │
│  Acknowledgments      July 1859                              │
│  Endnotes             August 1859                            │
│  Bibliography      Gold Fever                                │
│  Appendix A           Boulder Diggins                        │
│                       Staking a Claim                        │
│                    Back to Farming                           │
│                       Homesteading  └─────────────────┘     │
│                                                              │
└─────────────────────────────────────────────────────────────┘
```

Chapter links page.

the thumbnails are clickable links unless you explain. Also post a warning about large file sizes so that readers are prepared for how long a full-sized image may take to download. Oftentimes, large images will take a minute or two to appear in a web browser making the viewer believe that nothing is happening and close the window prematurely.

File Formats

Save full-sized images as smaller thumbnails using the "for the web" setting in your image editor, or at 72 ppi because the monitor cannot display an image at any higher resolution anyway. While web browsers will recognize and display TIFF, BMP, JPG, GIF and PNG files, you will achieve the best quality with the fewest compatibility issues if you stick to JPG or PNG. Use PNG if you want to maintain a transparent background if the image is an icon or a logo, for example, with sharp lines and distinct areas of color. Use JPG for photographs, maps or illustrations. Play with the image format for your documents to see what gives you the best results. Typically, documents that are fairly clean, with easy-to-read handwriting will look fine as a JPG.

Animation

While you can include animated graphics, such as animated GIFs or flash animations in your online book, please do so sparingly. Flashing or rotating graphics have fallen out of fashion and tend to annoy readers.

There are many ways, however, to create an animated slide show if you have a lot of images to share. Some of the most common website building software have simple plugins that create slideshows, or you can use stand-alone software such as Adobe Flash to create a file that plays like a video. Microsoft Movie Maker comes pre-installed on most Windows machines or is free to download. Macs have iMovie which is similar. Both iMovie and Movie Maker create web-ready video slideshows.

Another option is to find (or purchase) a flash gallery where the slideshow is already built, you just add the images. Search for "free photo gallery download" on the Internet and you will find hundreds of sites with flash galleries to download. One you have a flash gallery filled with images, upload it to the server and create a link to it in the navigation of the website.

Screen Captures

Screen captures for use online are similar to those used in eBooks. Zoom in to make the image bigger than you plan to use as a final size. Then reduce the physical size of the image to the optimal size you want displayed online without adjusting the resolution since the captured image will already be at screen resolution.

Book Cover Image

Use your book cover image in the banner or in the right-hand column of the page. To keep pages loading quickly, convert your book cover image as you would any other image for the website. If you use a thumbnail, you can link it to a larger image, if you wish.

Video

If you have video, you may want to use a thumbnail or link to take readers to a full-screen version of the video. If you create a "channel" on YouTube, you can store your video files there (saving server space that you may have to pay for), and YouTube will give you the code to bring the video into your website. You will copy and paste the code into the page on your website where you want the reader to play the video.

Audio

Audio files can also be large. If you can use your audio as the soundtrack behind a video slideshow, you can create a video and load it on YouTube as well.

Building a website to display your book is relatively easy if you are willing to learn to use an HTML editor or your ISP's online web-building tools. Many website-building options are drag and drop, which makes building a website easy. If you plan the navigation carefully, it will be obvious to the viewer what he or she should do next. Confusion is the nemesis of any website.

Most website options have ample room for text and images, which means you may be able to display more images on a book's website than in a printed book.

If you can keep the amount of text on any one page short enough that an average reader can finish in ten to fifteen minutes, readers will come back again and again to read what happens next in the story.

Chapter 17

Converting a Print Manuscript to Blog

One of the biggest advantages to publishing a book using a blog, is that the software is simple to learn. If you can create an email, you can create a blog post. Similar to a website, you will need a place to host your blog and blogging software to create it.

One disadvantage to publishing a book using blogging software is that you have to be ultra organized in order for the reader to understand how to move through the book, since there will not be any page numbers, only titles and the categories you assign to each post.

Creating a Blog

There are three ways to establish your own blog—you can obtain a free blog, install blogging software on your own website, or pay for a hosted blog.

Free Blogs

Free blog are available at the following websites—among hundreds of others:

- Blogger (www.blogger.com)
- WordPress (www.wordpress.com)
- Weebly (www.weebly.com)
- Tumblr (www.tumblr.com)

Install Blogging Software on Your Own Website

WordPress allows you to install their software on your own website. You can download the WordPress software on their developer site (www.wordpress.org). Once you have the files downloaded, use an FTP program to upload the files to the space your ISP has reserved for you on their server.

Hosted Blogs

Another alternative is a hosted blog. Hosted blogs are not free, although they have the advantage of: a little more control over how the blog looks; advanced features not available on free blogs; and better protection from spam comments.

Hosted (paid) blogs are available at one of following websites:

- Typepad (www.typepad.com)
- Squarespace (www.squarespace.com)
- Ghost (www.ghost.org)

Domain Names

Most blogs are assigned domain names as subdirectories of the blogging company (i.e. www.NewEnglandHenrys.WordPress.com). You can use your own domain name for your blog, however, by registering a domain with an ISP or registrar, and "pointing" the domain to your blog. That way, an address such as www.yourfamily.blogspot.com, becomes www.yourfamily.com. Consult with your ISP or registrar for instructions.

Building a Blog

The biggest benefit to using blogging software is how easy they are to set up and add information. Most blogs have a dashboard where you will make changes. Withing the dashboard you can change how the blog looks, create pages or posts, and organize images.

Themes

Most blogs come with easy-to-install themes. The themes will govern the look and feel of the blog. You should be able to scroll through a gallery of themes. Once you choose, you simply apply the theme.

Each theme has different features, and some are customizable so that if you want to add a search feature, for example, you can. Many themes allow you to change the colors, the fonts, the number of columns, and add widgets. Widgets are mini-software programs that perform functions such as a clock, or a date calculator. One widget most blogs offer is a search feature. If you include a search box, you may not need an index. The dashboard in the following example is from WordPress.

Organization

Blogs place the most recent post (information) at the top so that readers can see the latest contribution first. This is a benefit for on-going blogs, but a challenge for a book published on a blog. Most blogs have two tools that organize—the blogroll (list of posts) and categories.

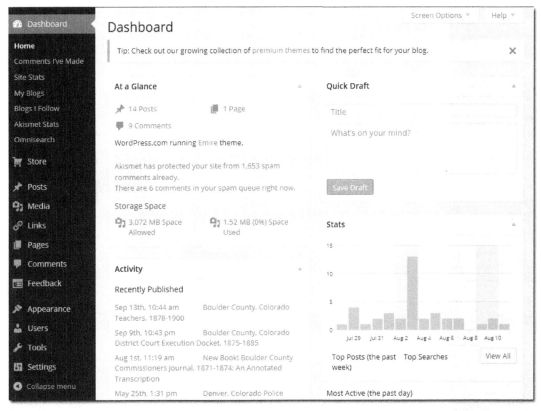

WordPress dashboard.

The blogroll (also called Recent Posts) lists the posts as they come in, so the titles of the posts will appear first at the bottom, last at the top. You can use this to organize the book if you post the entire book in reverse order, so that the end of the book appears at the bottom of the list and the beginning of the book appears at the top. The blogging software will create this list for you. This method is fine if you are planning to put the entire book up at once. It is problematic if you publish a post or two at a time, and readers are following your blog like they would a social media site. In this case, the story must be told in order from beginning to end.

The categories feature is another way to organize, and one that you have more control over. Each post can be given a category, which can be used to alphabetize the titles in order. This is the better method if you want to post a bit at a time, and have readers follow the blog as you update it. The categories feature is best if you want to maintain the blog as an online book long after you have finished posting to it. The finished list of categories will work like a Table of Contents.

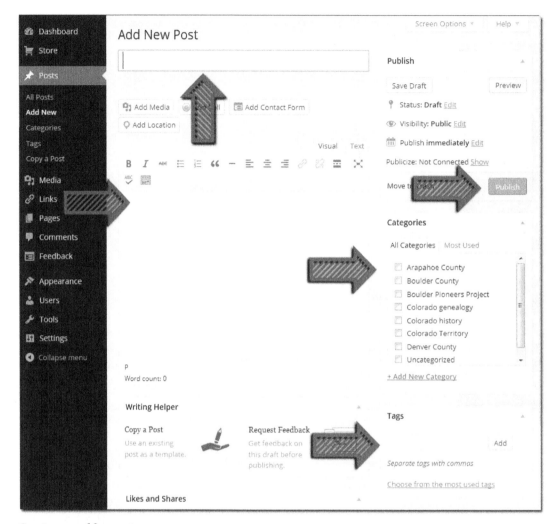

Create a new blog post.

Pages or Posts

Most blogging software allows you to create pages and posts. Posts are placed in a column, one on top of another with the most recent post at the top. Pages are static, more like traditional web pages. One option, is to ignore the blogging feature entirely and use only the static pages to organize your book. Another option is to put the front and back matter on pages and publish the stories of the book as posts.

Creating a Blog Post

If you can use email, you can blog. Many of the features are the same. In the example, you will see arrows pointing to:

The title. Use the title to get the reader's attention. Most blogs will compile the headlines into a list of "recent posts." That means, the list will be in order of what you posted most recently. This feature, unfortunately, is not particularly helpful to keep the book in its proper order.

The main body. Use the main body box for your text. Try not to make the post too long, or readers will have to scroll and scroll to reach the end. The longer the post, the more difficult it will be to keep reading until the end. Should a reader stop and want to come back later, he or she will have to reestablish his or her place in the text, which may not be easy unless you use subheads or other way points (images or strings of asterisks) within the text.

Categories. Use categories to organize the book. Each category will appear in the side bar of the blog. As long as you name your chapters so that they will alphabetize in the right order, your readers will not have any trouble knowing which link to click next.

  For example:
101 Uncle Friedrich goes to war
102 Aunt Mazie goes to work
103 Pop buys a car

You could start each post from Chapter One with a one (1), for example.

Keywords. Keywords help search engines categorize each post so that people who are searching for information on your family can find it. This is one way for readers to find your book. Keywords do not have to be single words. They can be phrases. Use commas to separate your keywords (or phrases). The following are suggestions for keyword phrases:

Surname (e.g. Clark family)

Surname plus genealogy (e.g. Clark genealogy)

First, middle and last name (of the person featured in the post (e.g. William Theodore Clark)

City, County, State where the story takes place (e.g. Linden, Perry County, Tennessee)

Subject or the key idea of the story (e.g. Tennessee Soldiers Civil War).

Publish. The publish button sends the post to the Internet. Most blogs also allow you to schedule posts, so that you can create a handful of blog posts, but only display them on the Internet every few days. It is one way to entice readers to return to the blog.

Plug-Ins

Developers have created plug-ins for many blogging platforms, many of which are free. Plug-ins for blogs, in many ways work like widgets in other platforms such as interactive books or your desktop. There are plug-ins for calendars, security, calculators, content importers, news feeds and even a few genealogically-driven plug-ins such as GEDCOM importers and pedigree chart generators. One caution about adding plug-ins, however. Plug-ins are created by interested developers. The developer may not be interested enough in the future to keep the plug-in working as the blogging software updates and changes.

Image Basics for Blogs

Preparing images for your blog is similar to preparing them for a website with a couple of exceptions. It is not as easy to use a small thumbnail to link to a full-sized image, and images may look best if they are kept under 500 pixels wide.

Media Gallery

Most blogs keep images organized in a media gallery. You can add images, animations, audio, or video to a post or a page once the item is loaded into the media gallery. Because video and audio files can be very large, you may have limited space to store these files. If you can upload your video (or audio as the soundtrack to a video) to YouTube, you can insert a link to the video on any blog post.

File Formats

Save images for blogs using the "for the web" setting in your image editor, or at 72 ppi because the monitor cannot display an image at any higher resolution anyway. Most blogs will accept JPG, GIF and PNG files. JPG tends to be best for photographs, PNG for logos or illustrations that have transparent backgrounds.

Book Cover Image

If the theme allows it, use your book cover image in the banner or as a thumbnail image in the column just below the search function. That way, it will be visible every time a visitor comes to the blog.

The biggest benefit to using a blog to display your book is the ease of establishing and adding to the blog. Blogs are dynamic and you can fill the posts with images which readers appreciate. The downside is how organized you have to be to create categories or title names so that the automatically generated categories list or blogroll (recent posts) will alphabetize the posts in a way that is obvious to the reader how to proceed from the beginning to the end of the book. If you can break up the stories into small bits and pieces and give each an appropriate title, using a blog is a fairly easy way to publish a book online.

Chapter 18

Converting a Print Manuscript for Social Media

One advantage to publishing on a social media site, is that there are so many users. Undoubtedly many of your family members are users. The nature of social media means your stories will become available to a large audience.

Social media sites are easy to use. They are very similar to blogging in that you create posts and pages, upload images and there are easy tools to invite cousins to see what you have posted.

There are two ways for viewers to find your posts. They can come to your fan page and see all of your posts, or they can like your page, and your posts will be delivered to them on their personal newsfeeds.

Social media sites have the same disadvantage as blogs in that you have to be organized enough to post the stories one at a time, in order. Because readers may be following your posts, you cannot load them in reverse order as you would on a blog to make the blogroll (list of posts) display the book in its proper order. On a social media site, readers will be following the book as it appears, so they need to read the book in order from start to finish.

Unfortunately, readers who discover your book sometime in the future after you begin posting may enter in the middle of the story. They will have to visit your fan page, and scroll to the bottom to start reading from the beginning.

Genealogywise (www.genealogywise.com), is a social media site for genealogists. Since your book is a family history, this may be the best place to host your social media book.

Today, Facebook is the largest social media site with close to a billion users. It was not the largest social media site in the past and may not be in the future. For this chapter, however, I will use Facebook to demonstrate how to set up a fan page for your book.

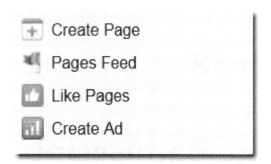

Create Page link.

Creating a Fan Page

In order to create a fan page, you must have a personal page. Create a personal account on Facebook and login.

In the left-hand column there will be an icon and link to Create Page. Click on the link.

Facebook wants to know what type of page you are creating. If your book is for family and friends, choose entertainment. If the book is for sale, choose Brand or Product. If you plan to post information about your publishing company as well as your book, choose one of the company page types.

Building a Facebook Fan Page

Once you answer the questions to establish your book or company's fan page, you will be able to customize it.

Add Header Images

There are two types of images that will be seen at the top of your page. The small square image is your fan-page profile picture. The profile picture will appear every time you post to the fan page.

In the example (right), the small square image of the buffalo is the profile picture. The largest size for a profile picture is 500 x 500 pixels. On your fan page, the profile picture will display at 180 x 180 pixels. In posts, it will appear as about a half an inch square. The profile picture is too small to show your book cover effectively.

You are also allowed a larger cover image that appears at the top of the fan page behind the profile image. (This is not referring to your book cover image. In this case, cover image is the term social media sites use for the largest image at the top of your page.) Use this image to showcase something about the contents of your book. Show the book cover or just the title and subtitle prominently, along with your name as the author and the website address where viewers can purchase your book. You can upload an image as large as 1200 x 450 pixels, but it will display as 851 x 315 pixels. If you submit an image smaller than 851 x 315 it will be stretched to fit the space, and may not look good.

Manage the Page

In the panel just below your cover image you will find the tools to create posts and handle other tasks. On the navigation bar you will find:

Facebook profile image (small square) and cover image (larger rectangle).

Timeline. This is the default view and will show all of your posts, the most recent at the top.

About. Answer questions about your book on the About page.

Photos. You can look through all of the images you post in this section. You can also arrange images into albums if you prefer.

Likes. This will show you who has "liked" your page. Once you start gathering "friends" on your personal page, you will be able to invite them to like your book page from an easy-to-use widget in the left-hand column that will show the person's picture, their name, and an invite button. Click the button and the person will receive an invitation. Do not be shy. Ask people to "like" your book's page.

Create a Post

At the left edge of your timeline, below your cover image, you will find a box where you can do the following:

Status. Your status is the same as a post on a blog. Put your text in the box that reads, "What have you been up to?" One way to help search engines find your posts on social media is to use a hashtag (# followed by words describing your post). Put a hashtag or two at the end of each post such as #YourBookTitle;

#YourName (as the author); #Subject (the post's subject); or #Location (related to the post).

Photos. You can add photos or video to each post.

Offer, Event+. This button allows you to do three things: post an offer, announce an event, and publish a milestone. An offer is a mini-ad. You will be charged for the ad, but it is one way to offer a deal on your printed book, for example. If you are speaking about your book, that's a good reason to use the event feature to announce the talk. Use the milestone feature, if there is something in particular you wish to note, perhaps when the first book sells, or the 100th.

Image Basics for Social Media

Preparing images for social media is similar to preparing them for a blog. Most images on social media sites look best if they are kept under 500 pixels wide.

Photo Albums

Every image you add will appear in your photo albums, whether you add them to an individual post, or directly to an album. You can create photo albums to categorize your images as you add them.

File Formats

Save images for social media the same way you would for a blog. Social media sites will accept JPG and PNG files. JPG tends to be best for photographs, PNG for logos or illustrations that have transparent backgrounds.

Book Cover Image

Upload your book cover image as one of your first posts. That will add it to your photo album and timeline.

The biggest benefit to using a social media to display your book is the incredible reach social media has across the globe. Social media has avid fans who use the sites daily because the news feed is dynamic. If you can break up the stories into small bits and pieces and give each an appropriate title, using social media is another easy way to publish a book online.

Note: The examples are taken from my Facebook page for the Boulder Pioneers Project (www.facebook.com/Boulder.Pioneers.Project). If you are researching early pioneers in Colorado, please come join us.

SECTION 5

While I believe that if you can do the research, you can also publish your book, you may not want to do it all yourself. The goal in this section is to help you negotiate the best deal and ask the right questions of a professional who can help you complete your book project.

Chapter 19

Working with a
Scanning Company

If the task of scanning hundreds of photographs, film negatives or slides seems overwhelming, contact one of the many companies listed on the Memory Preservation Coalition's website (memorypreservationcoalition.org). The coalition is a non-profit group dedicated to helping individuals preserve and archive documents and photographs.

One idea I particularly like is having a scanning service come to you. This idea was launched by Scangaroo, which has been acquired by Gen-Arc Digital Estate Scanning (www.gen-arc.com). They use mobile scanning labs to come to your home so that your important photographs, documents, scrapbooks or video never leave your possession. They also offer cloud-based digital asset management meaning you can store your family documents and photographs so that they can be shared with generations to come, assuming the company stays in business.

Another option is to contact FamilySearch about their Worldwide Photo Scanning and Preservation Initiative. The Mormon Church has teamed up with Kodak and E-Z Photo Scan (ezphotoscan.com), to equip a few of their Family History Centers, their central library in Salt Lake City as well as a center in Riverton, UT with high-speed, high-resolution scanners. Look for one of their "photopalooza" events or find out whether the Family History Center in your area offers photo scanning.

There are also local companies who can scan photographs, or convert older forms of analog film into modern digital video. A company that specializes in memory preservation, however, may be better than the local photo shop.

National Archives Standards

Before you hire a scanning company, ask whether they follow the guidelines prescribed by the National Archives for handling your photographs or delicate documents. You would not want an item damaged by careless handling.

File Size and Format

Make sure you have the images scanned at the largest size you think you will need to make a reprint or to include in your printed book. You may have images of different sizes to scan, so if you want all digital images large enough to create a full-page image in your book or a large photo reprint, be specific about that requirement.

Be clear about what file format (JPG or TIFF) you need. Most scanning companies will return files as JPGs. Unless you have a compelling need for TIFF images, JPGs will work for a printed book, an eBook, and any use you can think of online.

Bound Items

Ask about scanning photographs that are glued into photo albums. Photo albums often require special handling in order to scan, so these items may cost more. If your photo albums are bound or such that they will not lay flat on the glass for scanning, ask whether the company could re-photograph, or whether they have the kind of equipment used to scan open books. Book scanning equipment may be better for the uneven surfaces in a scrapbook than a flat, plate scanner.

Slides and Film Negatives

Ask about scanning slides and film negatives. Make sure the slides or film will be scanned at a resolution high enough to create a digital image large enough for your biggest need. Often slides and negatives are scanned at a standard 4000 dpi resolution which will yield an image of 3622 pixels by 5320 pixels for the average slide that measures 23mm x 34mm. This image size is large enough to produce a photograph of 12" x 17" at 300 dpi, which is large enough for most book projects unless you are planning an oversized coffee-table book.

Video Transfer

You may have other media that you want made into digital images or video transferred to a modern DVD—VHS, VHS-C, 8mm, Hi8, Super8, mini-DV or other formats.

Most film or tape to digital video transfer is done at a standard resolution, and the transfer is done in one piece—the length of the original film to a single video clip.

If you need still digital images from your video, work with the technician to create a list based upon time stamps. You may also need to ask for frame-by-frame images over several seconds in order to obtain the best still from video where the subjects are moving. This may cost a bit more, but is more likely to generate a useable image than a single shot.

If you need stills at higher resolution, that process is more difficult because the film must be marked and stopped in order to adjust the resolution upward. The technician will likely make the complete transfer, then rewind the film and start and stop at each place where you requested a digital still from the film. Again, this may cost a bit more, but if you need a high-quality, high-resolution digital image from a family video for your book, it may be worth the money.

Restoration or Retouching Services

Ask about photo retouching services. Most scanning companies offer basic retouching services, and some offer advanced retouching services for photographs that are badly faded or damaged. For most old photographs, even a bit of dust and scratch removal, color correction, sharpening, adjusting the saturation or correcting for over- or under-exposure is well worth the trouble and expense.

Much of this, however, can be done in your own image editing software. If the photograph requires extensive digital restoration such as fixing tears across people's faces, or removing color shifting caused from mold, expect to pay more. If the only photograph you have of one of your ancestors needs major restoration, the cost may be less important than having the image.

Write a Formal Proposal or Contract

Write a formal agreement detailing the work you want to have done, the cost, when you are to deliver the items to the company (or the date the company's scanning equipment will come to you), and when the scanning will be complete. Include the file type and how the images will be given to you—thumb drive, external hard drive, archival DVD, through a file sharing service, or in permanent cloud storage that you can access at any time.

Chapter 20

Working with a Photographer

You may need photographs for the book that you are unable to take for yourself, obtain from family members or from a helpful local volunteer. In this case, hire a photographer or license a photograph taken for other commercial uses.

Find the right photographer for the job. If you want a group picture of the entire family, or candid photographs taken during a reunion, find a portrait photographer—someone who specializes in people pictures.

If you need location photos, look for someone who shoots photographs for advertisements in the area. That photographer may have images not previously sold to clients that he or she would make available to you, for a nominal fee or photo credit. If the photographer has to go somewhere on your behalf, however, be prepared to pay for their travel time as well as shooting time.

Studio Photography

Another reason to consider using a professional is if you need good studio photographs of your heirlooms. A commercial photographer should be able to shoot objects in their own studios, or can take their equipment to the location where the objects are, if heirlooms are too fragile or too big to be moved to the studio.

Portfolio

Before you hire, ask to see a portfolio. Many photographers have their portfolios online, so you may be able to find exactly the right photographer before placing a call.

Fees

Ask about fees and whether they include travel, time at the location and any cropping or alterations before the photographs are given to you. You will not need prints unless you want them. Many photographers make their money on print packages, not on the time they spend taking photographs. If you do not want prints, let the photographer know this up front. The photographer may be willing to adjust the fees and agree to provide only digital images.

Most photographers who photograph an event will charge for the time they spend at the location, not by the number of images they take. Be clear about this, however. You will not want to pay for time and two hundred images you cannot use, just because the photographer took them. You also do not want the photographer to limit the number of photographs taken. Even with a good photographer, one quarter to one third of the shots taken will not be great photographs.

File Type and Resolution

Most photographers today shoot in resolutions much higher than what is needed for print production, so resolution should not be an issue. Ensure, however, that the photographer will deliver images in the largest resolution and size you need. In most book projects, that is the book cover image.

Location Images

If it is a location you need an image of, tell the photographer that you want a local landmark, for example, to use for your book cover. A good photographer will know to take shots from different angles, but it does not hurt to be specific. If you want a blue sky in the background, for example, in order to put your title in that space, say so. If possible, show the photographer a book cover with an image similar to what you want, so the concept for your book cover is clear.

Capturing an Event

If the photographer is to capture a family event, be specific about the images you want. Give the photographer a schedule of activities and a list of the people you want photographed. You may need to provide a spotter—someone who is familiar enough with the family to point out who is who on the shot sheet.

Consider asking for establishing shots—shots of the location where the event is taking place. Ask for close-ups as well as group shots, candids as well as staged or portrait shots.

Make sure the photographer is familiar with the event location. Schedule a site inspection with the photographer to discover any lighting issues, obstacles or distracting backgrounds to avoid while taking the photographs.

Deadlines

Set clear deadlines. Unless you have an upcoming family reunion where you would want the photographer to be present, wait until the manuscript is nearly finished to send a photographer to take location photographs for you. The only exception to this rule is if the time of the year makes a great difference to the quality (or subject) of the images. If you want a clear shot of a building, for example, you may want the photograph taken in winter.

Copyrights

Do not make a big issue about copyrights unless you are willing to pay more to make the photographer give them up. Portrait photographers expect to make their money on packages of prints, although many photographers are willing to take a higher event fee in exchange for giving you ownership of the digital images outright.

If you plan to use the photographs for more than your book project, make sure you obtain the rights for other uses as well—on your website, in your eBook, a family reunion t-shirt or journal cover, photo souvenirs, and any other uses you can think of. It is unlikely that a photographer will deny you any extended uses of photographs of your family. But, it does not hurt to be thorough.

If you have permission to use a volunteer's photo for your book (from sites such as Findagrave or Panoramio), but want to use it for some of the extended uses listed above, ask permission from the photographer for those uses as well.

Payment

Ask about any extra charges so there are no surprises, and clarify how you are expected to make payment and when. Half of the total fee is common for a down-payment to secure the booking, with the final half due upon delivery of the photographs. Ask about album fees, overtime charges, or any special handling of the images that may not be included in the quoted price.

Cancellations

Cancellations can be problematic. If you have to cancel, be prepared to pay at least part of the photographer's booking fee unless the cancellation is made well ahead of time. Unfortunately, there may be a reason for the photographer to cancel. To protect yourself, require that the photographer has a similarly-qualified backup colleague who will fill in in the event of a cancellation, or that he or she pay any additional charges you may encounter in order to hire someone at the last minute.

Write a Formal Proposal or Contract

Use a formal proposal to indicate the photographs you want and how you want them delivered to you—on a thumb drive, an external hard drive, an archival DVD, or through a file sharing service. Make sure deadlines and dates of events are clear. Include all prices and payment terms. State what uses the photographer is allowing you, and be specific about what happens if either you or the photographer cancel.

Chapter 21

Working with an Illustrator

Working with an illustrator is a bit different than working with a photographer. Because of the artistic nature of the work involved, illustrating often takes far longer than taking photographs. If you want one-of-a-kind illustrations in your book, build extra time into your publishing timeline.

Hire the right illustrator for the job. Illustrators have their own styles, although many illustrators can work in different media, such as pencil, pen and ink, or watercolor. Some illustrators create only computer-generated images. Find a style that you like, then choose an illustrator who can create the images you want. Use the same illustrator throughout the book so the style is consistent.

Portfolio

Ask to see a portfolio. Many illustrators have their portfolios online, or they can point you to other books they have illustrated. The illustrator may have worked on a book that is available commercially, and has an online preview.

Fees

Ask about fees and be specific about the size and resolution of the digital images you need. A professional illustrator should be able to advise you how their artwork will look best in a print publication, whether by scanning the originals or photographing them. There may be additional fees if the illustrator must engage a studio photographer to create a digital image of their art.

Deadlines

As with hiring other professionals, be specific about what you want and make your deadlines clear. Ask for a set price per illustration, and inquire about any extra charges so there are no surprises. Clarify how you are expected to make payment and when. Illustrators often require payment in installments as the illustrations are in progress, rather than half before and the balance after an event as you would pay a photographer.

Copyrights

Copyrights may be a more complicated issue with an illustrator than with a photographer because of the time it takes to create illustrations. You may wish to use the illustrations for other purposes, such as on social media, on your website or in your electronic book. If you have a reunion coming up, you could use the illustrations on giveaway items such as t-shirts, tote bags or mugs. Negotiate the rights to use the illustrations in other ways or at least leave open the possibility for uses in the future.

Cancellations

If you must cancel, be prepared to pay at least part of the fee unless the cancellation is made well ahead of time. If the Illustrator cancels, you can expect a full refund of any fees you have paid. In your agreement, ask that the illustrator pay any additional fees you encounter as a result of his or her cancellation if you are up against a deadline to finish the book.

Write a Formal Proposal or Contract

Use a formal proposal to indicate the illustrations you want and how you want them delivered to you—on a thumb drive, an external hard drive, an archival DVD, or through a file sharing service. Make sure deadlines are clear. Include all prices and payment terms. State what uses the illustrator is allowing, and be specific about what happens if either you or the illustrator cancel.

Chapter 22

Working with a Cover Designer

If you feel you cannot design your own cover, hire a cover designer. Ask about the designer's experience, however, since cover design is a specialty, and most graphic designers have never designed a book cover. Most book packagers, however, either have cover designers on staff, or use freelancers who are familiar with book cover design.

Take a look at Book Cover Archive (www.bookcoverarchive.com). This website offers a gallery of book cover designs. Show the prospective designer four or five styles that you like, but be open to suggestions.

In addition to cover ideas, bring along a two or three paragraph synopsis, to help the designer understand the content. The cover design should complement the content.

Portfolio

Ask to see the designer's book cover portfolio. Evaluate the full covers, front, spine and back, to make sure the designer is familiar with the elements needed for a commercially-available book.

Estimate

Ask for an estimate. Most cover designers will offer two or three designs, plus two rounds of revisions before you start paying more than the initial estimate. You may even find that the cover designer has a few standard layouts that you can choose from to save money. Include a do-not-exceed price in the agreement, so the designer cannot go wild with changes before you have a chance to revise the estimate.

Deadlines

Make your expectations clear and set firm deadlines. Let the designer know when you will have a final page count, and when you expect the final cover finished once the page count is given. The designer should have the cover essentially ready, needing only a few minor adjustments once the page count is final.

File Type and Resolution

Let the designer know what type of file and resolution you need (usually a PDF) and any special instructions provided by your book printer. In addition, ask for web-ready book cover images in the different sizes you may need—an eBook version (600 pixels x 800 pixels), online bookstores (Amazon's requirement is a cover of 1880 pixels x 2500 pixels), and a small thumbnail 90 pixels x 108 pixels (the standard cover size in Amazon's email promotions). Make sure the final cover looks good and that the title is readable, even at the smallest thumbnail size.

Write a Formal Proposal or Contract

Use a formal proposal to indicate how and when the cover should be delivered to you—on a thumb drive, an external hard drive, an archival DVD, or through a file sharing service. Make sure deadlines are clear. Include all services, prices and payment terms.

Chapter 24

Working with a Book Packager

Book packagers (designers) offer different layout and design services, including book design, typesetting, image preparation, cover design and in some cases indexing. Most book packagers will offer these services together or individually, depending upon your needs.

Interior Design

Provide your manuscript along with a few examples of layouts you like to the book packager so they can understand the type of book you have written, as well as your style preferences. Acquiring good examples may necessitate a trip to a library with a good genealogical collection. A trip to the local bookstore may not be helpful, as family histories are not often sold in bookstores.

Fiction tends to be formatted in a different way than non-fiction, although you will find good family histories formatted as fiction, such as The Family by David Laskin. Non-fiction formatting tends to be content specific, so choosing a nice-looking computer manual may not do you much good either. Using a good family history as your guide is probably best. A book designer who has worked with family histories before may have suggestions for you.

Most book designers will offer two to three designs plus two rounds of revisions before you pay more than the initial quote. The better you can explain or demonstrate what you want at the outset, the more likely the designer is to create what you are looking for in the first round of designs.

Typesetting

Most of the time, if you have a professional design your book, you will also have them typeset the book because you may not use the same software they use, so there would be no way to hand over the master layout to you. Before you submit your manuscript for typesetting, clean up any overlooked double spaces, tabs and section breaks. Then proofread carefully so you are not paying the typesetter to do that for you.

Print it out. A printout is a way to be sure that nothing is missing or misplaced in the manuscript files. You check it over first, then give it to the typesetter. If you find errors and make corrections to the manuscript, print a clean copy for the typesetter.

Image Preparation

You cannot prepare your images for the correct display size at the correct resolution until you have a layout in order to know how big or small each image must be in order to fit into the grid. If you have scanned the images at sizes larger than what will be needed, much of the hard work should already be done. Your book packager can then help you to correctly size the image for the book's layout.

Indexing

Not all book designers offer indexing services, although some do. Using a book packager or a professional indexer can be costly because he or she must read the manuscript in order to determine what should or should not be indexed, and that takes time.

Often called a poor man's index, you can make the job of indexing easy for a book packager by printing a copy of the final layout, and highlighting the items to be indexed. The highlighted copy along with a style sheet of how you want names, places and subjects indexed should be enough for your book packager to take care of the indexing for you.

Another option is to mark the index entries for yourself in your word processor. Index tags from Word import into InDesign, for example, and most book designers accept Word documents. Before you spend the time to index this way, make certain that the book packager can import your index tags.

Cover Design

Every book should have a cover worthy of the work it took to write it. Book packagers offer cover design services, or you may want to use a cover designer—a graphic artist who only designs covers. Either way, he or she will need to know whether the book will be available for sale. Commercial books have different requirements than books solely for your family's enjoyment. The elements of a book cover meant for commercial sale are described in Chapter 10: Cover Design for Print.

The cover will be the last part of your project finalized because spine width is dependent upon the final page count and the paper used, which may be different from printer to printer. In most cases, you will receive a template from your printer after you have a final page count, so that the dimensions and spine width are correct in the template. The designer can assemble the elements ahead of time and make final adjustments to the file when the page count is known.

File Formats

Most book packagers can work with any type of file format generated by one of the common word processors (.doc, .docx, .wpd) as well as plain text files (.txt) or rich text files (.rtf). Most word processors will also convert their native file formats to something more common such as a Microsoft Word file, if that is what the designer prefers.

Ask before converting anything. Converting to a plain text file will eliminate all of your formatting. Converting to a PDF is not helpful either, since PDFs are not easily re-formatted.

Portfolio

Before you ask about cost, look at the designer's work. You want to make sure that he or she has experience preparing books for a printer. Many book packagers have an online portfolio or can send you examples.

Another option is to hire someone who is looking to create a portfolio piece and is willing to do whatever it takes to finish the job to your satisfaction—at a lower price. Students and people who are learning the craft are often willing to work for much less than established book designers.

Cost

Book packagers charge for some services by the piece (image preparation), other services by the page (typesetting), and a few services by the hour (indexing). If you would rather have the designer give you a bid for the whole project, they will need to know the approximate page count and number of illustrations. They will set limits on the number of designs and revisions they will give you on the interior and cover. If you reject the initial round of designs all together, you may have to pay an additional fee to see more designs.

Write a Formal Proposal or Contract

Once you have a cost estimate from the designer, write an additional proposal making your expectations clear about what work will be taken care of by the designer, and what you are responsible for providing to him or her. Include firm deadlines and a do-not-exceed price—the price beyond which you cannot go.

Chapter 24

Working with an Indexer

Most family histories do not need the services of a professional indexer. You know your material as well as any indexer could. Professional indexing is often necessary for complex non-fiction or scientific works, but you should be able to either create the index yourself as you typeset, or be able to work with your book packager to do so.

Portfolio

A professional indexer should be able to give you the titles of the books he or she has indexed, and an electronic copy of an index or two.

What to Include

Your index should include every name mentioned in the book, along with the names of groups or institutions. Include place names that are significant to the story. The indexer may be able to suggest subject headings to you, since subjects are more commonly what professional indexers categorize, rather than names.

Fees

Professional indexers charge either by the page, or by the hour. If your indexer does not have much experience, pay by the page. Pay by the hour, only when hiring an accomplished indexer. Using a professional indexer can often run as much as book packaging or editing costs. If you have to choose, put the money into editing first, then into the layout and design. Leave the indexing for last.

Final Layout

A professional indexer must work from your final layout—with all of the typesetting in place and pages established—in order to create an accurate index. Before you give the final layout to the indexer, make certain all revisions or corrections have been made. Then, print a final copy.

After the indexing is complete, if you make revisions to the text that alters on which page the indexed words appear, you will pay dearly to have the indexer make corrections.

Write a Formal Proposal or Contract

Use a formal proposal to indicate how the index is to be returned to you or your book packager—as a Word document, or unformatted plain text document. Make your expectations for the index and deadlines clear. If you have agreed to pay by the hour, include a do-not-exceed price to keep the indexer from running wild with your budget.

Conclusion

I am confident that if you can do the research and follow the steps outlined in this guide, you can publish your work in print, electronically or online.

If you choose to publish electronically, let me encourage you, once again, to publish at least a few copies in print and to distribute those copies to the major genealogical collections around the country so that your hard work will be available to other interested researchers for generations to come.

If you are just beginning, I trust you are inspired enough to pick a project to publish. In fact, I hope to have inspired half a dozen projects you cannot wait to begin, and caused many more ideas to tumble around in your imagination.

If the research is underway but the writing is not yet complete, I anticipate that you will reach out to family members and others who can be of assistance to gather photographs, information, and stories you may not have heard.

If you have inherited a box of documents or photographs, my aim was to motivate you to begin scanning and organizing, sharing with family, and preparing the images for when you are ready to lay out your manuscript.

If the research is sitting in your computer yearning to bust out of the bytes and into the hands of family members, I trust that you believe that you *can* publish.

About the Author

Dina C. Carson has been involved in publishing and genealogy for more than two decades. She brings her experience with all phases of book publishing to help first-time self-publishers create quality family or local histories that are both believable and achievable.

She is the coordinator of the Boulder Pioneers Project, a comprehensive look at the original source documents for Boulder County during the territorial period (1858-1876) and is the author of more than a dozen annotated indexes of Boulder County source materials.

She lectures frequently to genealogical, historical and philanthropic societies, gives workshops on publishing, pioneers and other topics, and is working with the Colorado State Archives on state-wide records indexing projects.

Although her formal education is in international law and economics, she owns Iron Gate Publishing, a publishing company that focuses on genealogy, local history and reunion planning. She is also a partner in Imagination Technology, a graphic design and marketing firm working with local businesses.

When she's not at a computer working on a publishing project, you can find her photographing the pioneer cemeteries of Colorado.

Bibliography

Ashford, Janet and John Odam. *Start with a Scan: A Guide to Transforming Scanned Photos and Objects into High-Quality Art, 2nd Edition*. Berkeley, CA: Peachpit Press, 2000.

Blatner, David and Glenn Fleishman, Steve Roth. *Real World Scanning and Halftones: The Definitive Guide to Scanning and Halftones from the Desktop*. Berkeley, CA: Peachpit Press, 1998.

Bringhurst, Robert. *The Elements of Typographic Style*. Point Roberts, WA: Hartley & Marks, 2008.

Carter, David, ed. *Big Book of Design Ideas*. New York, NY: Harper Collins, 2000.

Cohen, Sanda and Robin Williams. *The Non-Designer's Scan and Print Book: All You Need to Know About Production and Prepress to Get Great-Looking Pages*. Berkeley, CA: Peachpit Press, 1999.

Ctein. *Digital Restoration from Start to Finish*. London: Elsevier, 2010.

de Bartolo, Carolina. *Explorations in Typography: Mastering the Art of Fine Typesetting*. 101 Editions, 2011.

Evans, Poppy. *Designer's Survival Manual: The Insider's Guide to Working with Illustrators, Photographers, Printers, Web Engineers, and More …* . Cincinnati, OH: How Design Books, 2001.

Felici, James and Frank Romano. *The Complete Manual of Typography: A Guide to Setting Perfect Type*. San Francisco: Peachpit Press, 2002.

Hendel, Richard. *On Book Design*. New Haven: Yale University Press, 1998.

Krause, Jim. *Color Index—Revised Edition*. Cincinnati, OH: HOW Books, 2010.

Krause, Jim. *Color Index 2*. Cincinnati, OH, HOW Books, 2007.

Lee, Marshall. *Bookmaking, 3rd Edition: Editing, Design, Production*. New York: Norton & Co., 2004.

Lupton, Ellen. *Thinking with Type: A Critical Guide for Designers, Writers, Editors and Students, 2nd Revised and Expanded Edition.* NY: Princeton Architectural Press, 2010.

Masterson, Pete. *Book Design & Production: A Guide for Authors and Publishers.* El Sobrante, CA: AEonix Publishing Group, 2007.

McClure, Rhonda R. *Digitizing Your Family History: Easy Methods for Preserving Your Heirloom Documents, Photos, Home Movies and More in a Digital Format.* Cincinnati, OH: Family Tree Books, 2004.

Pantone Graphics. *Formula Guide: Solid Coated & Solid Uncoated.* Carlstadt, NJ: Pantone Graphics, 2014.

Steinhoff, Sascha. *Scanning Negatives and Slides: Digitizing Your Photographic Archive.* Santa Barbara, CA: Rocky Nook, 2009.

Tally, Taz. *Avoiding the Scanning Blues: A Desktop Scanning Primer.* Upper Saddle River, NJ: Prentice Hall, 2001.

Wheildon, Colin. *Type & Layout: How Typography and Design can Get Your Message Across—Or Get in the Way.* NY: Strathmoor Press, 1995.

White, Jan V. *Great Pages: A Common-Sense Approach to Effective Desktop Design.* London: Serif Publishing, 1990.

Williams, Robin. *The Mac is not a Typewriter, 2nd Edition.* San Francisco, CA: Peachpit Press, 2003.

Williams, Robin. *The Non-Designer's Design Book, 3rd Edition.* San Francisco, CA: Peachpit Press, 2008.

Williams, Robin. *The Non-Designer's Type Book.* San Francisco, CA: Peachpit Press, 1998.

Index

Order Form

If you borrowed this copy from a library or would like to order a copy for a friend or family member, please send a check or money order to: Iron Gate Publishing, P.O. Box 999, Niwot, CO 80544. Our books are available online to institutions through Lightning Source, to individuals at Amazon.com and on our website:

www.irongate.com

Set Yourself Up to Self-Publish: A Genealogist's Guide
   ISBN 978-1-879579-99-6 $19.95 + $5.00 S&H

Publish Your Genealogy: A Step-by-Step Guide for Preserving Your Research for the Next Generation
   ISBN 978-1-879579-62-0 $24.95 + $5.00 S&H

Publish Your Family History: A Step-by-Step Guide to Writing the Stories of Your Ancestors
   ISBN 978-1-879579-63-7 $24.95 + $5.00 S&H

Publish a Local History: A Step-by-Step Guide from Finding the Right Project to Finished Book
   ISBN 978-1-879579-64-4 $24.95 + $5.00 S&H

Publish a Memoir: A Step-by-Step Guide to Saving Your Memories for Future Generations
   ISBN 978-1-879579-65-1 $24.95 + $5.00 S&H

Publish a Biography: A Step-by-Step Guide to Capturing the Life and Times of an Ancestor or a Generation
   ISBN 978-1-879579-66-8 $24.95 + $5.00 S&H

Publish a Photo Book: A Step-by-Step Guide for Transforming Your Genealogical Research into a Stunning Family Heirloom
   ISBN 978-1-879579-67-5 $24.95 + $5.00 S&H

Publish a Source Index: A Step-by-Step Guide to Creating a Genealogically-Useful Index, Abstract or Transcription
   ISBN 978-1-879579-68-2 $24.95 + $5.00 S&H

Publish Your Specialty: A Step-by-Step Guide for Imparting Your Research Expertise to Others
   ISBN 978-1-879579-76-7 $24.95 + $5.00 S&H

CPSIA information can be obtained at www.ICGtesting.com
Printed in the USA
LVOW03s0306081014

407785LV00004B/9/P